C000253056

Health, Wealth

&

Hypnosis

The way to a beautiful life

Gail Marra

Copyright © 2020, Gail Marra

All rights reserved. No part of this publication may be reproduced, distributed or transmitted in any form or by any means without permission of the publisher, except in the case of brief quotations referencing the body of work and in accordance with copyright law.

The information in this book should not substitute professional medical advice. The reader is advised to always consult a medical practitioner.

ISBN: 978-1-913479-23-7 (paperback)
ISBN: 978-1-913479-24-4 (ebook)

That Guy's House
20-22 Wenlock Road
London
England
N1 7GU
www.thatGuysHouse.com

Dedication

To my beautiful family, my soul group, my inspiration, my reason for living, you know who you are.

And to you Dear Reader, for having the courage to explore the phenomenal power of your subconscious mind

Foreword

Hypnotherapy has been part of my life for over 40 years, since I was 22-years-old. Over the years, I have come to know the benefits and the power of hypnosis, and like an old friend, it has helped me with a range of challenges from giving up alcohol and dealing with anxiety, to focussing on my writing and directing as a filmmaker.

A good hypnotherapist is hard to come by, and I had been looking for one for over ten years. I was hoping for the best when I met Gail, and she was so personable, empathetic and knowledgeable that I took to her immediately. Gail has since helped me work through a number of personal issues, but perhaps the most remarkable is that although I had been living in Spain for ten years when we met, and I had taken Spanish classes for many of those years, I failed to speak it. In fact, I could barely utter a word. After just a few sessions with Gail, I went back to Spain, opened my mouth and spoke Spanish properly for the first time. My Spanish teachers and friends marvelled at my sudden fluency. The vocabulary and grammar had been there all along, locked inside my subconscious, but I had just been too frightened to speak, for fear of making a fool of myself. Gail and her hypnotherapy unblocked all of that.

This book, *Health, Wealth and Hypnosis,* demystifies what hypnosis really is; the 'look into my eyes,' swinging pocket watch and stage tricks are not what hypnotherapy is all about. This is a book of its time, and Gail's explanation of hypnotherapy and how it fits in with the current use of meditation and mindfulness for mental health is enlightening. It offers a trio of practises for mental health, if you like, using the power of suggestion to help you overcome whatever challenges life throws your way.

There are a great many helpful exercises inside this book; the garden exercise in particular is wonderful. The 7 / 11 breathing exercise, which Gail uses in her sessions, has become a part of my daily life, to be used anywhere, anytime. This book is an enjoyable and easy read, a work that you will keep close to hand and refer to often.

Barbara Rennie

Screenwriter and filmmaker

Contents

A Very Brief Introduction

'You never get a second chance to make a first impression.'

If there is validity to this saying, then I have just a few meagre seconds (or perhaps as little as a millisecond) to make a good impression on you, my potential reader and literary companion. And so, I will start by asking you a question: what was it that attracted you to this book? What grabbed your attention? Could it have been the image, the font, the title or the lure of discovering your hidden potential? Moreover, have I made a good enough impression to encourage you to read on a little further?

You see, most of us would like to believe that all of our choices and decisions are carefully and meticulously thought through. Of course, the big ones often are, but decision-making may well be a process handled largely by our unconscious mind. In an experiment conducted by the Max Planck Institute for Human Cognitive and Brain Sciences in Leipzig, Germany, researchers found that it was possible to use brain signals to predict which option participants would take seven seconds before they consciously made their decision. Interesting stuff.

So, here we both are, hopefully about to buddy-up on a journey of sorts into the powerhouse that is your subconscious mind. Another question: if you were to conduct your own market research and ask 100 people what they really want out of life, what do you imagine they would say? There would no doubt be variations, but I wonder if it might essentially come down to one or all of the following: to be healthy, to be wealthy and to be happy (not necessarily in that order).

Research has shown that being happy helps to promote and maintain a healthy immune system. It reduces stress levels, decreases the risk of heart disease by lowering blood pressure, helps moderate pain and can even help you to live longer. When we are in a state of happiness, our brains release a heady cocktail of feel-good chemicals. We are flooded with endorphins, serotonin, oxytocin and dopamine, and in these moments, we feel as though we don't have a care in the world. All of our worries, problems, stresses, anxieties and even pain seem to just float away, and everything is wonderful (for a while).

Wouldn't it be incredible if you were able to switch those chemicals on at will?

Well, you can.

Allow me to introduce myself. I am a clinical hypnotherapist with a busy clinic in Central London, a career path that has proved to be a vocation rather than a job. I am an ardent student of Psychology and a lover of science, and I have an insatiable appetite for research. I believe in the unlimited potential of the human mind. I believe that we all have the power to regain and take control of our lives, and to overcome self-imposed barriers and self-limiting beliefs that can hold us back and prevent us from living our best lives.

Over the past 30 years, I have researched, studied, practised, tried, tested and taught all manner of self-improvement and personal development techniques, occasionally to the point of obsession, but never to the point of exhaustion. My own journey has been, and continues to be, as wonderful as it is challenging, and like many, I have made gaffs and blunders along the way, but my curiosity and zest for life has never waned. I have seen too many remarkable transformations that people have made in their lives to deny the power of the subconscious mind, which to me would be nothing short of ignorance.

We the people are evolutionary creatures. We evolve, we learn, we grow and we develop, not just physically, but also cognitively and emotionally. We modify, we adapt, we can transform our lives and effect change, and therefore, self-improvement must surely be our birth right. We are the only living creatures on this planet who possess the ability to change the course of our lives! Think about it. A lion can't choose to go vegan, a caterpillar has no choice but to become a moth or a butterfly, fish can't choose to live on the land and an apple seed can't choose to become a grapefruit, yet we humans can choose how to live our lives. We can choose to change.

The universe, our planet and everything on it is in a state of continual motion, and so in practise, it is quite impossible to stand still. So, why do so many of us feel stuck?

This book is more than a self-help book. It is an easy-to-follow guide that I hope will help you to understand and learn how you can reprogramme your subconscious mind to recognise old patterns of behaviour that no longer serve you, and negative beliefs that play over and over like a broken record, holding you back from experiencing the life you desire.

You may choose to read this book from beginning to end over the course of a few days, revisiting some of the exercises and chapters that matter to you most, or perhaps you will dive into it randomly, depending on how you feel on any given day or time in your life. Feel free to use this book however you wish, although, if you are determined and motivated to change, improve or reboot your life, I encourage you to practise the exercises regularly, and to have fun with them along the way.

Your subconscious mind is phenomenal. When you learn something new, your brain creates new neural pathways, and when repeated enough, they become an automatic response. The reason you don't have to remind yourself to breathe or tell your heart to pump blood around your body, and why you don't have to concentrate on walking and talking at the same time, is because all of these things and so much more are under the control of your subconscious mind. It's not just responsible for your automatic functions, either. Your subconscious mind is the place where all of your deepest-held beliefs and behavioural patterns are wired and stored.

So, in the same way that you are not continually aware of breathing, your heart pumping or the act of walking and talking at the same time, you are also most likely to be unaware of repetitive thoughts, such as *Things never work out for me*, *I never have enough money*, *My relationships always fail* and *I can never be successful or happy*.

The jury is out regarding exactly how long it takes to break a habit, or for a new habit to become automatic. However, what we do know is that the more we practise something, the better we become, and the better we become, the less we have to think about doing it.

I hope this book will prove to be a valuable asset to you, and one which may just turn out to be the most 'well-thumbed' book you have ever owned.

The choice, as always, lies with you.

Chapter One

Look into my eyes

'You use hypnosis not as a cure, but as a means of establishing a favourable climate in which to learn.'
– Milton H. Erickson, psychiatrist and psychologist

The way in which the medical community views hypnosis is changing, and its use in mainstream medicine is increasing. The Royal College of Midwives not only now recognises hypnobirthing courses, but also funds training for midwives. Many anaesthetists use hypnosis as part of their approach, while dentists use it to calm anxious patients. At my own clinic, doctors, surgeons and consultants regularly refer patients to me in order to help them heal better, recover quicker, manage pain and feel more in control of their condition and their treatment. In addition to these existing practises, researchers are also now asking if hypnotherapy could be a potential solution to the opioid crisis.

In 2017, a study led by two university neuroscientists, David Spiegel and Heidi Jiang, measured brain activity in participants under hypnosis using magnetic resonance imaging (MRI). The research team noted three distinct changes in those hypnotised:

1. A decrease in activity in the part of the brain that diverts your attention and brings things into conscious awareness.

2. An increase in the connections between the areas of the brain that process and control what is going on in the body.

3. A disconnection between someone's actions and the awareness of their actions.

(Source: *Cerebral Cortex, Volume 27, Issue 8*, August 2017, p. 4083–4093)

I think Dr Spiegel sums hypnosis up very well in stating, 'It's a very powerful means of changing the way we use our minds to control perception and our bodies.'

Therapy of any kind given on a face-to-face basis is of course the preferred route, however, unlike counselling and most other forms of psychological therapy, hypnosis can be taught and practised in the comfort of your own home. I often record therapy sessions for clients, so that they can listen at their leisure between visits to clinic. Some sessions are designed specifically to be listened to as you go to sleep at night. As you drift off, you are in a hypnotic trance (Theta), and positive suggestions or affirmations will act as your nightly marinade. I recommend that my clients listen again first thing in the morning, when their subconscious mind is operating at its optimum (Alpha), which is the gateway to the subconscious mind.

In a nutshell, hypnotherapy is a form of therapy used to reprogramme the subconscious mind. During hypnosis, your mind and body are in a heightened state of learning, making you more susceptible to positive suggestions for self-improvement or behaviour modification. The goal is to put the subconscious and conscious mind in harmony, which in turn helps give you greater control over your behaviour, emotions and physical wellbeing.

As I mentioned earlier, clinical hypnotherapy is not like the performances you see in stage shows; there are no swinging pocket watches or purple capes involved. In a clinical hypnotherapy session, you are in control the entire time. You will hear the suggestions made to you, and you will be able to remember them after the session. Hypnosis cannot do or change anything that you resist or disagree with.

While we are here, let's dispel a few myths about hypnosis:

1. You cannot get stuck in hypnosis. This is quite impossible.

2. You do not become in any way unconscious or semi-conscious.

3. You cannot, at any time, be made to do things you do not want to do.

4. You are totally aware of yourself and your surroundings at all times.

5. You do not go to sleep.

6. You are not in anyone's power, and nobody can take control of you.

7. You can leave the hypnotic state whenever you want.

8. You cannot lose your mind.

9. Hypnosis cannot permanently remove memories or thoughts from your mind.

10. You will not suddenly blurt out your deepest darkest secrets.

11. Hypnosis cannot bestow psychic abilities or supernatural powers.

12. Hypnosis cannot make you act against or abandon your moral code.

13. You do not say or do 'funny things' (unless, of course, you choose to).

Hypnosis is a truly natural state, and it is therefore perfectly safe. Many of the clucking chicken images are the result of hypnosis's forefather, Franz Anton Mesmer (1734-1815), hence the word 'mesmerised.' Mesmer believed that there was an invisible force, a cosmic energy, that could be harnessed by one person to influence another's behaviour. While his theory was incorrect, the techniques he used were effective, and consequently they were picked up on and developed over the years for therapeutic and medical purposes, with even Sigmund Freud employing hypnosis techniques. However, it wasn't until during the mid-1900s that hypnotherapy as we know it today began to take shape.

What does it feel like to be in hypnosis?

The experience of a hypnotic trance feels similar to countless other moments in your life, where you have been absorbed in a good book or movie, lost in thought or engrossed in music, driving or meditating. Once you enter a state of hypnosis, your body and your mind feel calm and relaxed, and your subconscious mind will be open to positive suggestion for change. Hypnosis is a willing state, so if you *want* to experience it, you are a good candidate, but if someone is trying to hypnotise you against your will, it simply won't work. For that reason, if you are extremely sceptical of its efficacy, or if you are frightened of it, it may not work for you.

Hypnotherapy, either on its own or in conjunction with conventional mainstream treatment, has been shown to be effective in the management and improvement of so many issues, both psychological and physiological, including:

- Stress

- Anxiety

- Panic attacks

- Phobias and Fears

- Preparation for surgery and other medical procedures

- Pain management and pain relief

- Gastro-intestinal disorders, such as irritable bowel syndrome (IBS)

- Cardiovascular disorders, such as high blood pressure

- Dermatological disorders, such as eczema and psoriasis

- Gynaecological disorders, such as PMT and dysmenorrhoea (painful periods)

- Infertility

- Tics, stammers and obsessive-compulsive disorders (OCD)

- Sleep disorders

- Weight control

- Smoking cessation

- Breaking unwanted habits

- Post-traumatic stress disorder (PTSD)

- Improving sport performance

- Improving academic performance (e.g. controlling exam nerves)

- Public speaking

- Building self-confidence and self-esteem

- Positive thinking

Hypnosis is not magical or mystical, and while it has not been proven to cure disease, it has been proven to reduce the symptoms of a wide variety of psychological and physiological conditions.

Self-hypnosis

Most people are under the impression that in order to get better, do better or make problems disappear, they need to enlist the assistance of someone else, be it a doctor, a nurse, a chiropractor, an osteopath, a herbalist, a homeopath, a surgeon, a psychiatrist, a pharmacist or anyone else who happens to hold a professional degree or certification. Putting ourselves in the hands of a person of authority tends to make us feel secure and more confident of finding a solution to our ailments. As a result, you may find yourself taking a pill, potion, tonic or vitamin, rubbing on ointment, having a massage, drinking alcohol or smoking, vaping or sourcing recreational drugs. These days, we have moved into the ominous era of self-diagnosis. We seek cures and remedies via the likes of Dr Google, and act upon the advice of testimonials, forums, bloggers, YouTubers and reviewers. Back in the day, we would have referred to such courses of action as 'asking the bloke down the pub,' and you yourself might have searched and read dozens of articles, joined self-help groups and like-minded sufferers associations, and become a medical researcher in your own right. We have instant access to virtually every piece of information known to man, but is this a blessing or a curse? Perhaps it's a bit of both.

I often wonder what it would be like if we treated people with little more than a good dose of motivation, a dash of willpower and a sprinkle of persistence. Could we actually learn to heal ourselves? Now, I am not suggesting we dispense with medical professionals and medical science, far from it. Medical advances and breakthroughs are helping to keep us all living longer, but what I am suggesting is that perhaps we should consider if there is more we can do for ourselves in order to sustain healthier, happier and longer lives.

Let's take a look at antidepressants and anti-anxiety drugs, aka SSRIs. SSRI stands for Selective Serotonin Reuptake Inhibitors, and includes drugs such as Prozac and Diazepam. These drugs, and drugs like them, act on the neurotransmitter serotonin, one of your happy chemicals that helps regulate mood. Now, in order for an antidepressant, and many other drugs for that matter, to be effective, you must have a complementary receptor. In other words, the drug needs something of the same ilk to stick to. If you are taking a serotonin uplifter, you need to already have serotonin in order for the synthetic version to uplift it.

Like any other drug, SSRIs can have side effects, which may include:

- Nausea

- Weight gain

- Decreased sex drive

- Tiredness and lethargy

- Trouble sleeping / insomnia

- Dry mouth

- Blurred vision

- Constipation

- Dizziness

- Anxiety

Hold on a minute, 'anxiety?' A common side effect of a drug to treat anxiety and depression is anxiety? That little nugget aside, all those other potential side effects would go a long way towards causing... you got it, anxiety and depression.

(NB: the above is not intended as a substitute for professional medical advice, and is based solely on my personal experience and opinion. As a reader, you should always consult a physician in matters relating to your health, and particularly with respect to any symptoms that may require diagnosis or medical attention.)

I digress. Now, back to self-hypnosis.

Because your subconscious mind does not deal in words per se, it does not make distinctions between negative and positive phrases, such as 'I am' or 'I am not.' If you are repeating or focussing on phrases like, 'I am not afraid of spiders,' or 'I am not going to feel anxious,' your subconscious will translate this as 'I am afraid of spiders,' or 'I am going to feel anxious,' and dutifully emit the necessary chemicals and signals from brain to body in accordance with your statement of intention. This is called the Law of Reverse Effect, and when your conscious thoughts are in conflict with your subconscious, your subconscious (which is responsible the vast majority of your brain's activity) reigns supreme.

And so, be mindful of the suggestions / statements / affirmations / thoughts that you focus on, both in meditation and in hypnosis, and be sure to be clear about the things you want, rather than fixating on the things you do not want.

Exercise 1

(NB: unless otherwise stated, the only tools required to enjoy the exercises in this book will be:

1x your good self, 1x an open mind and 1x a quiet space.)

Nice to meet you

1. Find a safe, quiet space to sit or lay down, ideally at a time when you are unlikely to be disturbed. These moments are all about you; there is nothing you need to do but relax and unwind. Anything that needs to be done can be taken care of later. If you need to attend to anything urgently while you practise, you will attend to it calmly and effectively.

2. Close your eyes as soon as you feel ready.

3. Now, focus on your breathing. Notice where you are breathing from and take your breath deeper. Breathe in through your nose and out through your mouth. Slow it down and control it, allowing your lungs to expand deep down into your stomach.

4. Now, bring your attention to the top of your head and begin to relax each and every part of your body, all the way down to the tips of your toes. Let each part relax even deeper on every out breath. Each time you exhale, think of the word, 'RELAX.'

5. When you have relaxed your entire body from the top of your head to the tips of your toes, begin to think of a place that makes you feel wonderful, peaceful and serene. It can be anywhere at all. Let your imagination take you there. It could be somewhere familiar or somewhere created in your mind's eye: a forest, a tropical beach or a mountaintop; beside a river, lake or stream; in a meadow or a field; on a ship, a rowing boat, a bicycle or a jet ski; anywhere, anytime...

6. When you find yourself in your place of peace and tranquillity, notice if you are looking out from behind your own eyes or observing yourself from a distance. There is no right or wrong way to use your imagination / mind. Let your subconscious mind guide you.

7. See what you see, hear what you hear and feel what you feel. Notice any fragrances on the breeze or in the air. Using all of your senses, allow yourself to become fully immersed in the experience.

8. Now, wherever your imagination has taken you, find a place to sit. You are safe and relaxed here.

9. In the stillness, notice a beautiful image of someone approaching. This person radiates such love and warmth that the feeling seems to envelop you. How wonderful it feels to share this peaceful place with this person.

10. As you look into the eyes of the person sitting next to you, recognise that the person is you. Look at yourself not as in a mirror, but in physical form. Smile and embrace whatever action feels right in this moment.

11. Now, begin a conversation with your Self. Talk about anything that comes to mind. This is a time to ask questions and listen to the answers. Talk about the things you really want out of life; where you would like to go and things you long to do, accomplish and experience. Talk about the past, clearing the air as you talk things through. Laugh or cry together as you reminisce. Make plans, discuss changes and talk about anything you choose. This is, after all, a very private conversation between aspects of one beautiful soul.

12. When you are ready, take a deep breath in, and when you exhale, allow your eyes to open.

13. Stretch.

14. Smile.

Hypnosis is like a system reboot for the mind. When your computer is running slow, you clean it up; you remove old programs that are no longer useful, you scan for viruses or threats, you check for updates and reorganise your desktop, removing or adding a few icons and perhaps changing your wallpaper. Give it a bit of a spring clean, an overhaul, and before you know it, it is running much smoother. If all that failed, would you give up? Toss your computer in the bin? Put it away in a drawer or in the attic to gather dust? More than likely, you would continue troubleshooting or enlist the help of an expert until you were satisfied with the way your computer was running. It's an investment after all, and no doubt you paid good money for it.

Your computer is replaceable, which means you could always go out and buy a brand-new one. You could bring it home, download all the things from your old computer that you need and would like to keep, and permanently delete any old programs that have become obsolete. The biggest and most complex computer that has ever existed, or ever will exist, however, is your brain. Your brain is not replaceable, it is irreplaceable. As investments go, your brain is priceless. It can become overloaded and in need of a clear out, a reboot or an upgrade. Your mind is miraculous, a gift, a treasure, and in the same way you would look after something that was precious and irreplaceable, you need to look after your mind. So, why wait until it needs attention? Why not look after your mind in the same way as your body, checking in with it every day to make sure everything is running smoothly?

When your mind is right, everything else follows.

Chapter Two

And breathe

Breath is everything. When you made your entrance into this world, everyone in the room held *their* breath until they were satisfied you had taken yours. Your first breath. That miracle moment you switched from taking in liquid to taking in air (oxygen, to be more precise); the most basic of autonomic functions, and something we usually take for granted. Immediately prior to your birth, your lungs were filled with fluid. They were not inflated. Within ten seconds or so of your glorious arrival, you gasped for air as your central nervous system reacted to the sudden change in your environment. The fluid that had been in your lungs either drained or was absorbed from your respiratory system. Your lungs inflated and began working on their own, delivering oxygen to your bloodstream and removing carbon dioxide with each exhale. You were breathing a bit faster than you will do as an adult, taking pauses between breaths and most likely making the odd gruffly sound as you breathed in and out through your nose and mouth, but the interesting thing here is that you will have been using your belly to breath. This is called abdominal breathing, and it is the most efficient and relaxed way of getting sufficient air into your lungs.

As you grow and develop, you will more than likely breathe into your upper chest. This way of breathing can place the body into emergency mode, triggering your 'fight or flight' response. Upper chest breathing is, of course, most useful in the event of danger or threat, as it produces the adrenaline and cortisol necessary for strength and speed. No surprise, then, that this breath is ideal in sport and competition, e.g. racing or sprinting, as it prepares the body for immediate action. However, if upper chest breathing becomes a regular pattern, the brain recognises low levels of carbon dioxide as being normal. Consequently, the body exists in a state of constant high alert.

In times of extreme stress or panic, you may *feel* as though you will stop breathing. You could become dizzy, experience blurred vision or even faint, but unless you have shuffled off this mortal coil, you will continue to breathe, although very likely using less than 50 percent of your breathing capacity, at least in most cases.

You might have heard the terms 'conscious breathing,' 'mindful breathing' or 'breathing manually,' which all refer to breathing with focussed attention. It may seem a little strange to think of breathing in this way, or indeed to practise breathing in this way, but I suggest you try it. Begin by focussing on your breath. Notice if you are breathing into your chest or into your abdomen, in and out through your nose or your mouth. Notice if you are taking deep breaths or shallow breaths, and if you are breathing slowly or quickly.

Conscious breathing encourages you to breathe deeper and slower, and so delivers more oxygen to your cells and organs. This method of breathing calms your mind, allowing you to think more clearly, make better decisions, digest food better, heal faster and have a stronger immunity to disease. Conscious breathing also helps you to process thoughts, feelings and emotions more effectively.

Sages and gurus of old have always recognised the importance of using breath as a way to induce a state of relaxation and deep meditation. Pranayama is the name given to formal practise of controlling the breath, and this is at the heart of all yogic exercise. Prana is a Sanskrit word for the universal energy that circulates inside of us, and which can be developed and channelled through controlled breathing.

Breathing consciously is also part of the ethos of mindfulness. Companies like Google, Nike, Apple, and Goldman Sachs have all been known to invest in mindfulness training for their workforce, and the Government here in the UK has invested public funds into studying the benefits of mindfulness in schools. Some 370 schools across the UK have been taking part in mindfulness exercises, relaxation techniques and breathing exercises to help them regulate their emotions. Small studies with offenders in the US found that mindfulness may help offenders to improve self-regulation, reduce negative emotions, reduce drug use and control aggression.

Mindfulness is about paying attention to (i.e. being mindful of) your thoughts and feelings without judging them. That is to say, being aware without wondering why or believing there is a right or wrong way to think or feel in any given moment. We will take a look at mindfulness in more detail later on in this book.

The following exercise is super powerful. In the space of just one minute, you can stimulate your vagus nerve and alter your brain's chemistry by releasing endorphins, serotonin, dopamine and oxytocin; your 'feel good' chemicals. Not to be confused with the *Vegas*, the gambling capital of the world, the term 'vagus' is derived from the Latin for 'wandering.' This is because your vagus nerve wanders from the brain into organs in the neck, chest and abdomen. Stimulating your vagus nerve triggers your parasympathetic nervous system – your 'rest and digest' – which is, by its very nature, the opposite of fight and flight.

Ready to check your breathing?

Exercise 2

All you need is the air that you breathe

1. Become aware of your breath. No need to force the breath or try to change it; just notice it. Notice the space that you are utilising in your body. Notice if your breath is shallow and quick or deeper and slower. Are you breathing in and out of your nose, your mouth or a bit of both?

2. Now, let your breath move and swirl around your body. Try visualising it as a shape or colour. Begin to enjoy the feeling of breathing manually, taking over the controls. Breathe in through your nose and out through your mouth. Try not to purse your lips, instead letting them part naturally, leaving just enough space to allow the air to pass through in a controlled manner.

3. Notice the difference in temperature as you breathe in and out. Notice how it feels cooler as you breathe in and warmer as you breathe out. Imagine the hairs in your nostrils swaying to and fro, like blades of grass blowing in the breeze. Imagine using your breath to blow away any busy or intrusive thoughts, a mental spring clean, if you like. An emotional detox.

4.   Take your breath even deeper. Open up your rib cage and push your stomach outwards as you breathe in, allowing your lungs to expand into the space. As you exhale, push the air out of your lungs using your abdominal muscles to push the air out from the bottom, consciously emptying your upper chest last of all.

5.   Now, start counting. Breathe in until the count of seven, and breathe out until the count of 11.

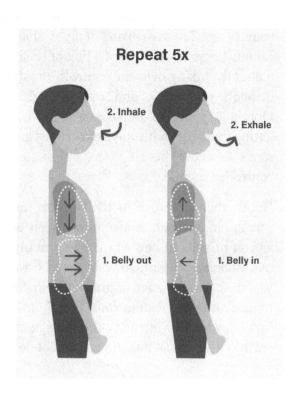

Five cycles of this slow diaphragmatic breath will trigger your vagus nerve and the secretion of your happy chemicals. I am sure you will agree that it is impossible to be angry and happy at the same time, or stressed and calm for that matter, and so by using this breath to produce those feel-good chemicals, you're telling your body to enter relaxation mode, aka 'Rest and Digest.'

(NB: an audio version of the 7/11 breathing technique can be found at my website: www.gailmarrahypnotherapy.com)

Chapter Three

A play on words

I have a bold statement to make. I disagree with the *Oxford Dictionary's* definition of 'Hypnosis.'

'The induction of a state of consciousness, in which a person apparently loses the power of voluntary action and is highly responsive to suggestion or direction. Its use in therapy, typically to recover suppressed memories or to allow modification of behaviour, has been revived but is still controversial.'

In my clinical practice, never has a single client lost the power of voluntary action, apparently or otherwise. In contrast to its dictionary definition, hypnosis is a state of focussed attention, and *hypnotherapy* is the use of this focussed state to facilitate a therapeutic outcome. Another way to look at hypnotherapy is to think of it as a guided meditation, where a trained therapist will help your busy conscious mind to quieten down, allowing the subconscious mind to open up and become more receptive to positive suggestion. I often liken the state of hypnosis to driving a car. During waking hours, your conscious mind is the driver, a chatty driver, a busy body, a road hog; thinking, planning, plotting and scheming, applying logic, doubt and reason to things that may not even be relevant, and judging them nonetheless. Your subconscious mind sits dutifully in the back seat, taking care of, well, everything else. In hypnosis, your subconscious mind is able to jump over into the front seat and take control of the wheel. Conscious mind is relegated to the back seat and autopilot is in control.

Now, as I have challenged the *Oxford Dictionary*, I would like to dip a toe into the field of neurology. Neuroscience tells us that our amazing brain has five brain wave states:

1. Beta
2. Alpha
3. Theta
4. Delta
5. Gamma (formerly disregarded)

Beta is your normal waking state, Alpha is a relaxed state, where you are at your most creative; Theta is observed during REM sleep, hypnosis and meditation, and is considered the frequency of the subconscious; Delta is the state of deep sleep, and then there is Gamma. Gamma is a frequency that science once referred to as 'spare brain noise,' at least until researchers discovered that it was highly active in people experiencing emotions such as deep love, gratitude and altruism. These days, there is growing acceptance that Gamma relates to expanded consciousness and a spiritual emergence.

If you have ever found yourself staring out of a window, daydreaming or having thoughts of flying off to a far-flung tropical paradise, or if you have ever been lost in a good book, engrossed in a captivating movie or driving somewhere you have driven to hundreds of times without taking any notice of how you got there, you have been in a hypnotic trance, or Theta brainwave frequency. A hypnotic trance is a natural state; one that we all experience many times a day. If we could bottle it, it would sit proudly on the shelf marked '100% natural and organic.'

Your subconscious mind is phenomenal. It accounts for 95% (possibly more) of everything that you are. It generates new thoughts and ideas, all of your choices and decisions, and everything that you have or will ever imagine. Your brain is a computer, you are the programmer and your life as it appears today is the direct result of all your subconscious programming. The things that you enjoy and that come easily to you, as well as the things you feel stuck with, are all there because you have a program that allows them to be there.

During the first seven years of life, we are mostly in a Theta frequency. The great Greek philosopher, Aristotle, once said, 'Give me a child until he is seven, and I will show you the man.' Up until the age of seven, we are literally downloading from the matrix, the mainframe, the motherboard, and so while we were busy downloading, who was writing the programs?

Parents, caregivers, schoolteachers, siblings, peers, television, YouTube, video games, social media and the like, that's who.

Let's simplify it further.

Imagine that at some point in your early development, someone who you looked up to saw a spider and became hysterical, screaming out loud, running about and behaving erratically.

Program: Response to spider = Terror.

A young person being told that life is unfair and a constant struggle, money is the root of all evil, without education you will amount to nothing, the rich get richer and the poor get poorer...

Program: Life = Hardships; unlikely to go succeed or go far.

A boy being told to 'Man up' or 'Big boys don't cry.'

Program: Showing emotion = Weakness.

The good news is that you can change, tweak or modify behavioural patterns. You can change bad habits, rid yourself of phobias, boost your immune system, lower your blood pressure, slow down your heart rate and change your brain chemistry, and thus your programming, at any age!

How?

Right up until the 1960s, the scientific community believed that changes in the brain could only take place during early development, and that by the time we became adults, the brain's structure was permanent. Today, research has demonstrated that the brain creates new neural pathways, altering existing ones to adapt to new experiences. This means that we can learn new ways of behaving and responding, change old patterns, outdated or indoctrinated belief systems, and even create new memories.

(Caveat: although brain changes are deemed improvements here, there are cases where the brain can be affected by psychoactive substances, disease or injury, all of which can lead to detrimental effects on the brain and behaviour. This is not a topic covered or explored in this book.)

Programming a young mind involves not just actions, but also words, and these words can have an emotional impact on the person receiving them. The words we use, and how we use them, create pictures in the mind. Regardless of the language spoken, words have negative or positive connotations depending on how they are put together in a sentence, how they are delivered and the meaning behind them. The words you speak to someone else will go through a set of processes, and the original meaning can often get lost. Misunderstandings occur, fights break out and people become estranged, bitter or angry. Negative words can make you feel sad, worthless and deflated. On the other hand, positive words – words of love, respect and encouragement – make you feel confident, proud and happy. Words matter.

Body language also matters. We can tell a lot from someone's facial expressions and their general body language. Clinical studies have shown that even very young babies can recognise faces and detect the emotion behind facial expressions. By the time we are five months old, we are able to match the image of an emotional expression with a corresponding vocal expression, and by the time we are five years old, we have the ability to decipher facial expressions at the same rate as an adult.

The ability to interpret words and cadence, recognise facial expressions and read body language is crucial for survival. We need to read other people, process the information and respond quickly if we are to know that we are in danger or under threat. Intonation and tone are extremely important when interpreting the spoken word. For example:

'You said THAT?'

'YOU said that?'

'You SAID that?'

The placement of the emphasised inflection determines how the message is likely to be received. 'Sticks and stones may break my bones, but names will never hurt me,' is an old rhyme that most will be familiar with. It is used to help children who are being bullied or put down to stand up for themselves, to become more resilient and take less offence. When we are offended or feeling put down, it makes us feel bad and it hurts, and this feeling is usually felt in the heart area.

Your heart contains neurons like those found in the brain. While this does not necessarily mean that your heart is capable of making decisions on its own, there are some interesting studies and branches of science currently looking into the role of the hearts 40,000 neurons and its network of neurotransmitters, to see how your heart communicates with your brain. You can find more information on this at https://www.heartmath.com.

You may have noticed how people will often place their hands on their hearts when being, or trying to appear, sincere ('Hand on heart!'). It's an automatic, instinctive inner knowing that tells us our heart is our centre, our essence, our spirit and our soul. It is no wonder that in the absence of logic or reason, we can often be led by our heart.

Your subconscious mind does not differentiate between a real event or an imagined one. This explains why when you recall something meaningful or feel excited or anxious about a future event, the emotion is felt in the heart area.

Exercise 3

Feel the Love

Have go at Exercise 2 before moving on to this exercise, and read the instructions over at least once in advance.

By using your breath to relax your body, you can lower your blood pressure, slow down your heart rate and change your brain chemistry. You have climbed over into the back seat of your metaphorical car and handed the keys over to your subconscious mind.

1. When you are ready, allow your eyes to close.

2. Start breathing slowly and deeply, in through your nose and out through your mouth.

3. Let your mind wander freely until you find something, some place or someone that gives or has ever given you a wonderful feeling; perhaps love, euphoria, happiness or joy in your heart. When you have that picture in your mind...

4. Make it bigger and brighter. See the scene as if you were looking at it through your own eyes. Be there. See what you see, hear what you hear and use all of your senses to relive or reimagine the scene as if it were happening right now in glorious technicolour.

5. Notice your heart rate, your breathing and your facial expression.

6. Inhale that good feeling; breathe it into every fibre, every nerve and every cell of your being. Hold it for a few moments.

7. Deep breath in, and on your next out breath, open your eyes.

Opening your heart in this way will set you up for the day. Imagine if you were to begin every day with a loving thought and a healthy dose of endorphins!

Chapter Four

Mind-body connection

Your body responds to your thoughts.

In the previous exercise, we demonstrated how your thoughts affect how you feel in your heart area. Your body responds to the way you think, feel and act. This is the mind-body connection.

Let's jump straight into another exercise.

You can either read the suggestions first, or you can enlist the help of someone else to read it aloud to you. It is a bit of fun, but significant.

Exercise 4

Get connected

I advise that you read the following steps in advance:

1. Make yourself comfortable.

2. Breathe in through your nose and out through your mouth. Pay attention to your breath. Breathe and deeply slowly.

3. Visualise yourself standing in front of a refrigerator. It could be your own, or even a big, shiny new one. Notice the colour of the fridge, the size, the shape and where it is positioned in the room. Become aware of your surroundings, notice where you are.

4. Reach out to touch the door handle and pull it wide open. On one of the shelves, you see a bowl of juicy ripe lemons. Notice the bowl itself. What it is made of? How many lemons are in the bowl? Become aware of the pungent, zesty fragrance as you reach in and take one of the lemons in your hand. Feel its weight; the texture and the temperature. Hold it up to your nose, breathe it in. Now take the lemon over to a chopping board, place it on the board and find a kitchen knife. The lemon rolls around a little, so steady it before taking the lemon in one hand and the knife in the other and slowly slicing it in half. As the lemon splits open and falls in two, it wobbles around before coming to a rest on the chopping board. The juices are running through your fingers and down your hands now, over the knife, the chopping board and the countertop. The pips pop out of the lemon, you tip your head back and raise the lemon to your mouth and squeeze the juice over your tongue. Your tongue responds instantly to the acidic juice, as it tickles the inside of your cheeks, your gums and the roof

of your mouth. It runs down your chin. It's cold, fragrant and your taste buds feel as though they are bursting with saliva.

5. Open your eyes.

How does your mouth feel right now? Are you salivating?

As I mentioned earlier, your subconscious mind does not distinguish between a real event or an imagined one, and simply produces whatever it is you need in order to deal with a given situation.

So far, we have looked at how, with the power of your mind, you can control the way you breathe, alter your brain chemistry, lower your blood pressure, create changes in your heart rate, stimulate your taste buds and feel calmer.

Now, let's take a look at the other side of pleasure.

How the body responds to pain

Pain is in the brain. And while pain is unpleasant, it exists for a reason. Pain directs our attention to an injury or a problem, so that we can take care of it and prevent further damage.

We think of pain as a physical sensation, but it has biological, psychological and emotional factors, too.

Chronic pain can cause negative emotions like anxiety, anger and feelings of hopelessness, which can all lead to depression. To treat pain effectively, we need to address the physical, emotional and psychological aspects.

Can you control pain?

In a word, yes. It is possible to control, manage and block pain.

We will now look at all three options.

__Pain control__

Research suggests that because pain involves both the mind and the body, changing the way you perceive pain can change how you experience it. Pain can also be influenced by your genes, emotions, personality, temperament and lifestyle. Pain can be influenced by past experiences, so if you have been in pain for a length of time and it has become an expected sensation, your brain will have wired itself to receive pain signals even when the signals are no longer being transmitted. It is the way in which your brain processes pain signals, and your beliefs about those signals, that lie at the heart of pain control.

Hypnobirthing is one example. In the UK, hypnobirthing, the use of hypnosis as an aid to natural childbirth, has become mainstream. Many NHS hospitals throughout the UK offer hypnobirthing classes as part of their antenatal programmes, which was unheard of when I was having my children in the 1980s. Back then, we had options as follows:

1. Grin and bear it

2. Gas and air

3. Epidural

4. Pethidine

5. Forceps

6. Suction

7. Caesarean section

Yours truly opted for the latter on both occasions, albeit, I would add, on medical advice. Often referred to as 'too posh to push,' the convenience of being able to organise one's diary, arrange childcare and return to work complete with power suit and shoulder pads might have been a contributing factor to the rise in C-sections during this period. However, today we are far better informed and are opting for more natural forms of pain management.

Most acute pain can be controlled to a large degree with the power of your mind. Physical pain has an emotional component, which means you always have some control over how you respond to it.

Hypnotherapy and self-hypnosis can alter your mood almost immediately, reducing stress, anxiety and pain intensity, but how?

1. Relaxation. The releasing of endorphins (more on this in a moment)

2. Distraction. Have you ever cut your finger and been so distracted with stopping the bleeding that you've forgot to think about how much it hurts? The pain usually comes after the wound has a plaster or bandage on it!

3. Reframing. When we use reframing, we can alter the perception of pain (e.g. from a burning sensation to a feeling of warmth, then cool and then cold)

4. Dissociation. With dissociation, you separate the sensation of pain from your physical body. You can visualise yourself from the other side of the room, seeing yourself as an observer. You can visualise the area that is causing the pain detaching from your physical body and floating away. Sound a bit abstract? Try it. You have nothing to lose, but possibly, much to gain

Managing chronic pain

There have been lots of studies focussing on the body's stress response to chronic pain. Apart from the obvious pain relief drugs that are readily available, one of the strategies for the treatment of chronic pain includes antidepressants. This is interesting to me, as antidepressants look to create an increase in serotonin, which we produce, and can boost, quite naturally. Serotonin is a neurotransmitter that helps regulate emotion. Serotonin lifts your mood, is the precursor to melatonin (the hormone that regulates sleep) and supports your ability to think clearly and to focus.

While serotonin has a dampening influence on the perception of pain, so do endorphins. Endorphins are peptides that stimulate the body's opiate receptors, which has an analgesic effect. The word endorphin comes from the words 'endogenous,' meaning from within the body, and 'morphine,' which is an opiate pain reliever. In other words, endorphins get their name because they are natural pain relievers.

You now know that you can produce endorphins, oxytocin, dopamine and serotonin by using abdominal breathing techniques, and so this should be your first port of call when it comes to managing pain.

There are also many other things you can do to boost your body's natural pain relievers:

1. Regular exercise

2. A healthy diet

3. Good quality sleep

4. Listen to music

5. Meditate

Hypnoanalgesia – blocking pain

Hypnos (Greek: 'sleep') + Analgesia (the inability to feel pain).

Hypnoanalgesia is the use of hypnotic suggestion to alleviate pain. Mind-body methods for medical and surgical procedures date back to the ancient Greeks and Egyptians, who used it for anything from limb amputation to cataract surgery. It was Santiago Ramón y Cajal, a 19th century Spanish neuroscientist, who published one of the first clinical reports on the use of hypnotic suggestion to induce analgesia during childbirth.

In January 2017, surgeons in Germany successfully conducted the world's first deep brain surgery using hypnosis instead of anaesthetic to control the patient's pain. The news rocked the world of neurosurgery and opened the doors to new innovation and new possibilities.

Alama Kante had a tumour surgically removed from her throat with local anaesthetic and hypnosis. Her surgeon, Professor Dhonneur, said that it was the first time a tumour had been removed using this technique, as the procedure would usually be carried out under general anaesthetic: 'The pain of such an operation is intolerable if you are fully awake. Only hypnosis enables you to stand it. She went into a trance listening to the words of the hypnotist. She went a long way away, to Africa. And she began to sing – it was amazing.'

Today, the clinical application of hypnoanalgesia is considered an effective technique for the reduction and alleviation of pain during surgery. It has been shown that patients undergoing surgical procedures under hypnosis report less blood loss during operations and a quicker recovery post-surgery.

My professional experience in the field of pain control and management

I have had the privilege of working with many wonderful clients over the years, helping them manage conditions such as fibromyalgia, arthritis and chronic fatigue, and to overcome symptoms of irritable bowel syndrome, dysmenorrhea, Lyme disease and idiopathic pain.

My work with cancer patients is particularly rewarding, as I help my clients to find ways in which to harness their inner resources to induce a state of calm, feel less anxious and more in control of their condition, treatment and prognosis. Clients have reported fewer side effects associated with chemotherapy and radiotherapy, such as a reduction or complete cessation of nausea and vomiting. My clients have also reported tremendous success in alleviating needle, cannula and blood phobias, as well as anxiety relating to hair loss. Alleviating fear and anxiety associated with cancer can help the nervous system become less reactive to it.

Pre-operative anxiety is something I see in clinic quite regularly. When clients learn how to calm their mind and then their body, amazing things happen. A few years ago, I worked with a remarkable client who was scheduled to undergo an awake craniotomy. This procedure is performed in the same manner as a conventional craniotomy, but with the patient awake during the operation. As frightening as this may sound, it is the preferred technique for operations to remove tumours close to, or involving functionally important regions of, the brain. The therapeutic approach I took in this instance was more 'hypnosedation' than hypnoanalgesia, as communication and response reactions were crucial to the success of the operation. We worked together regularly over a period of four-six weeks prior to surgery, using visualisation techniques to experience (as much as was possible) the entire procedure; every sound, every sensation and every visual. With guided imagery, my client's subconscious mind was primed and prepared as though the procedure had already taken place and had been a complete success. Furthermore, the speed of my client's recovery was a pleasant surprise for everyone on the medical team.

Hypnodontics – hypnotherapy in dentistry

Hypnosis is used regularly in many dental practices; certainly in the more forward-thinking practices here in the UK. You can ask anyone how they feel about going to the dentist, and the majority will probably get a shiver down their spine. Not many people enjoy going to the dentist, and a few will suffer extreme anxiety or dentophobia. Insignificant cavities that could easily be filled, but instead are left unattended, can lead to broken and rotting teeth, and the resulting pain can be excruciating and require invasive reconstructive work. In a not so distant past, the British were renowned for having bad teeth, with Austin Powers and his dreadful set of teeth being a prime example of how the rest of the world viewed our dental hygiene. Today, however, we are all expected to have clean, healthy, shiny white teeth. If your teeth are broken or discoloured, or if you have receding gums or halitosis, you may experience social stigma, which in turn can lead to isolation, depression and even agoraphobia, which in effect would be exchanging one phobia for another! In short, dentophobia is a common and very treatable phobia.

(NB: beautiful teeth produce a beautiful smile. And a smile produces... you've guessed it... Endorphins!)

Bonus Exercise

SMILE!

1. Expose those pearly whites (or shades of).

2. No matter where you are or how you are feeling right now, just SMILE. Not a grin or a smirk, but a great big toothy smile.

3. Let your teeth part.

4. Open wide.

5. Raise your eyebrows. You may feel silly, and it may even turn into laughter. A good belly laugh relaxes your muscles and relieves all kinds of tension and stress. Laughter boosts your immune system by increasing your immune cells and infection-fighting antibodies.

6. If you have a mirror to hand, use it.

7. Maintain silly face until mood lifts (even if only a little).

Chapter Five

Healing

'Healing is a matter of time, but it is sometimes also
a matter of opportunity.'
– Hippocrates

Pain is not just physical; pain can also be emotional. Emotional pain can manifest as physical pain, and physical pain can cause emotional pain. Add to this illness and disease, and you have yourself a heady mix.

Clinical studies have shown time and again that prolonged periods of stress have a negative impact on the immune system. When your immune system is compromised, your body is more open to illness and disease. Heart disease and circulatory issues, such as gastrointestinal problems and various types of cancer, have been shown to be exacerbated by stress. Depression, anxiety and post-traumatic stress disorder are just some of the emotional or mental health issues caused, or made worse, by stress.

Why?

Adrenaline, cortisol and noradrenaline (norepi-nephrine). These Three Musketeers are the chemicals (hormones) your brain produces when you are in fight or flight mode, or to be more precise, 'fight, flight or freeze.' The human body is designed to trigger its primal FFF response when we are in clear and present danger, under threat or feeling vulnerable. It is during times such as these that we need blood to flow to our muscles; we need sharp thinking and a massive boost of energy.

A typical example would be ancient man (or woman) coming face-to-face with a sabretooth tiger. Here, we have three scenarios: run from said sabretooth, freeze and hope it doesn't notice you or fight the beast and bring it home for supper. The human stress response is crucial here, as we would need to react swiftly, find strength and be quick about it. Competitive sports people need to summon the Three Musketeers when they are taking part in an event, a game, a match or a race. Adrenaline increases heart rate, elevates blood pressure and boosts energy supplies. Cortisol increases glucose in the bloodstream and enhances the brain's use of it, while noradrenaline does much of the above, but also increases blood flow to the muscles. The part of the brain responsible for unleashing these chemicals is the hypothalamus, which triggers the sympathetic nervous system (ironically named, as it is often less than sympathetic when called into action).

Imagine a gazelle grazing lazily upon the savannas of Africa. Gazelle is minding his or her own business when a pride of lions appears on the horizon. The gazelle stops in its tracks, ears and hackles up, and, sympathetic nervous system at the ready, it freezes. Aware that it has no chance of fighting, it flees for its life, and having outrun the lions (in this instance at least), the lucky gazelle returns immediately to grazing lazily upon the savanna. This is a prime example of nature's system working harmoniously.

Now, I am not suggesting that we humans have the brain capacity of a gazelle, only that this is how our stress response should operate in an ideal world. We do not live in an ideal world, however, and so it is understandable that our systems are a bit out of sync from time to time.

There are hundreds, and quite possibly thousands, of reasons why people become ill, and not all are connected with the mind. Nevertheless, science is continually finding evidence that the brain has the power to influence and indeed change the body's physiology.

Mind over matter

In ancient times, science was not needed to prove the power of mind over matter; it was an unwavering belief. There were shamans, witch doctors, medicine men/women, spellcasting, incantations, the calling of spirits and, of course, prayer to help aid the ailing. Even today, in some cultures, societies and religions, the power of belief, aka the power of the subconscious mind, is fundamental to curing disease and restoring health.

Let's say you have a papercut on your finger. Unless there is a condition present that stops the natural healing process, such as haemophilia, you do not get overly involved or concern yourself with the physical healing process. Other than perhaps a plaster or a dab with a wet tissue, you will probably not become emotionally involved in the process, either. You are in no doubt that the papercut will heal itself. You trust that your body will swing into action to stop the flow of blood; your blood vessel walls will narrow, platelets will rush to the site and protein in your blood will make the platelets stick together, which will form a clot that will plug the bleed. A scab will form, go crusty and, in no time at all, fall off – hey presto! What about the common cold? Unless your immune system is compromised, there will be no doubt in your mind that your cold will pass. It may be uncomfortable and irritating for a few days that seem to go on forever, but the question as to whether or not the virus will eventually pass seldom comes to mind. You trust your immune system to do what it needs to do in order to attack and fend off the virus. Your brain and your body invariably know what to do and when to do it in order to keep you alive.

So, when we are faced with something more sinister than a papercut or a cold, why do we begin to doubt that we can heal? I am in no way suggesting that mind over matter is all we need in order to heal and stay healthy – there are other factors to consider, not least advancements in medicine and medical research – but research has shown that how quickly or slowly we heal or recover has a direct correlation to our psychological state of mind.

The Biology of Belief, an inspirational book by biologist Dr Bruce Lipton, states that our cells, genes and DNA are manipulated by our mind, and so by definition, we can literally think our way to health. Dr Lipton's belief is that our genes do not control us, we control them. The field is known as epigenetics, of which Dr Lipton says: 'Between one-third and two-thirds of all healing is down to the placebo effect, not therapies, drugs or surgery. The placebo is just a sugar-pill – the patient is healed by the belief they'll get better: positive thinking.'

I will talk more about placebo later in this chapter.

The mind-body connection is nothing new. Right up until a few hundred years ago, most societies in the world treated the mind and body as a whole. It was only during the 17th century that the West deemed the two unconnected, claiming that body parts could be repaired or replaced without the mind having anything to do with it. Fast forward to the 21st century, and what had once been science fiction has now become a hard science, neuroscience.

The body is designed to heal itself, but you can enhance and accelerate the process with modalities such as mindfulness and meditation, and more specifically, hypnotherapy. By directing the subconscious mind to focus energy on a specific area in the body, you can tap into and precisely direct many of your natural resources.

Feeling is believing

There is a procedure called 'sham surgery,' which is when surgeons literally fake performing an operation, and while it is highly controversial and some may say highly unethical, the results have been quite astonishing.

There are certain rituals associated with surgery: hospital appointments, blood tests, instructions not to eat or drink, surgical gowns, the smell of surgical spirit, the brown tint of the iodine as it is applied to the skin, conversations among the surgical team, their uniforms, masks and gloves, the pressure felt during an incision, the sound of a drill, the reassuring words from the anaesthetist, staying overnight, hospital food, the scar and so on. All of these signals create a profound image in your mind, leaving you in no doubt that you are being, or have been, operated on.

In 2014, the BBC produced a documentary investigating the healing power of the mind. The documentary featured Dr David Kallmes, a well-respected radiologist from the Mayo Clinic in the United States, who regularly performed a procedure called vertebroplasty. Vertebroplasty is a procedure in which a special cement is injected into a fractured vertebra to relieve spinal pain and restore mobility. The procedure produced pleasing results, but what was more interesting was that whenever the procedure went wrong, patients still reported remarkable improvements. Dr Kallmes went on to design a trial where some patients would be given genuine vertebroplasty and some would be given a placebo. In this case, however, the placebo was not a fake pill, it was a fake operation, a sham surgery.

All patients were prepared in exactly the same way. They would all have been given the nil-by-mouth instruction (taste), then wheeled into theatre (visual) and given a local anaesthetic in the back (touch). The special cement was opened, which had an odour similar to nail polish remover (smell), and as the doctors at this point still did not yet know whether they were about to perform a real procedure or a fake, the chatter in the theatre was lively (sound). With all five senses activated, the patients' subconscious minds accepted the fact that surgery was about to take place, and that relief would soon follow. The results were truly amazing. Patients who underwent the real vertebroplasty and those who received the fake (sham) surgery all reported improvement.

You say placebo, I say nocebo

Most of us will have heard of the term placebo and the placebo effect, even if not so much in regard to sham surgery as the 'sugar pill.' This fake pill has no medicinal properties, yet it can produce a positive effect in a patient. Researchers use placebos in clinical trials when looking into the effectiveness of a new drug. In these trials, researchers give some participants a fake drug, some the real drug and some receive nothing at all. This way, the researchers can evaluate the overall effect of the drug treatment under study. As with the sham surgery, not informing participants or patients as to which drug they are taking raises a few ethical eyebrows, and so today we are seeing more 'open placebo' trials. In these trials, participants are fully aware that they are taking a placebo, and the results have been intriguing. A recent study revealed that people suffering with irritable bowel syndrome showed a greater improvement after being given an open placebo when compared to those receiving no treatment at all. Other research has shown that open placebo trials for conditions like arthritic pain and hay fever have also shown promise.

The archnemesis of placebo is nocebo. The nocebo effect is what happens when you are given a fake drug and told to expect a handful of dreadful side effects. These false side effects may include nausea, stomach cramps, itching, anxiety, sleep problems or loss of appetite. Participants in the nocebo group often begin to exhibit some or all of the suggested symptoms. The nocebo effect can also occur when a medical professional, or someone whose opinion you hold in high regard, tells you that a surgery or procedure could have negative results, as just knowing the risks could negatively impact your recovery. It is well documented that in some cases where patients have been given a poor prognosis by their doctor or surgeon, it has resulted in their premature death.

Hypochondria

Hypochondria is fearing that any physical or psychological symptom experienced will result in the diagnosis of a serious illness and possibly demise.

I know quite a bit about this subject, as I suffered with it myself in my early twenties. Looking back now, of course, I can see how it began and how it went on to manifest, so I will lay it out before you as best as I can:

1. Age 16: left school, left home and went to work

2. 16-17: worked hard, partied hard and experimented with soft drugs

3. 18: oblivious to responsibility, took out a mortgage and bought an apartment

4. 20: got married

5. 21: expecting my first child

6. 23: got a bigger mortgage to buy a bigger house

7. 24: filed for divorce

And so, it was during these early years, in my haste to grow up, that I became completely and utterly overwhelmed. Anyone who knew me back then would have told you that I was a happy-go-lucky, confident and ambitious young woman, who appeared to be in full control. I, too, would have told you that, but the truth was that I had taken on too much too soon, and I had no idea how to slow down.

I vividly recall the day I took my daughter to our regular mother and toddler group at the local church hall. On this particular day, a new mother joined the group, and as we chatted, she confessed to having just been diagnosed with a debilitating illness. This information hit me like a ton of bricks. My ears were ringing, my heart was pounding and I felt the blood rush to my face. How could this be? We are new mothers, are we not immortal? I could not stop thinking about this unfortunate woman; I just could not get her out of my mind. I wanted to know more about her, her illness and her symptoms, but I was too afraid (and too polite) to ask. Now, these were pre-internet days, and so the only way that I could get my hands on medical information was via the public library or my GP, and so for the next year or so, these were the two places where I spent much of my free time.

At the library, I would give my little girl picture books to look at and toys to play with while I scoured the medical reference section to see how my 'symptoms' compared with those of the people who had been diagnosed and since passed away from dreadful diseases. Finally, my GP, exasperated by seeing my name continually clogging up his diary, sat me down and tried to get to the bottom of what was really going on. I accepted a prescription for antidepressants, and I even took them for a short while, until I realised that the only reason I was not going to the library to look under 'diseases of the day' was because I had become too lethargic to walk there! Thankfully, after flushing the pills, I came through the troubled episode unscathed and have since lived on, obviously. It was around this time that my interest in psychology and mind over matter really peaked, and for that I am eternally grateful.

Exercise 5

Prepare to heal

1. Make yourself comfortable and close your eyes. Focus on your breath. Each time you notice your mind wander, acknowledge the thought, let it pass and bring your awareness back to your breath.

2. Notice the cool air going in through your nose and the warmer air coming out through your mouth.

3. Beginning at the top of your head, *imagine* relaxing your scalp. Relax your forehead and soften your brow. Let your entire face relax, allowing your teeth to part and your jaw to drop slightly. Relax your neck, imagining all the muscles, nerves and fibres in your neck softening. Imagine each and every vertebra down the spine relaxing, like a pianist stroking the keys of a piano, all the way down to your tailbone.

4. Now, take this feeling of relaxation through your entire body, inside and out, via every major organ, as well as your veins, arteries, capillaries and cells. Imagine your intestines cooling and being soothed, and your stomach and entire digestive system releasing excess acid and being replenished with a soothing elixir. Let your mind travel through your body, soothing everywhere and anywhere that remains tense or uncomfortable. Your body is loose and relaxed. Your subconscious mind is following your guided instruction, and in return it will release the chemicals and hormones necessary for regeneration, healing and calm.

5. Think about your immune system. What does it look like, this network of tissues, cells, and organs that tries to keep out germs like bacteria, viruses, fungi and parasites? Know that when your immune system senses something in your body that could be bad for you, it will trigger the release of cells that know exactly where the trouble is and how to attack it.

6. Imagine yourself tagging along with your immune system for the ride. Move through every area of your body, visiting your lymphatic system, white blood cells, spleen and bone marrow. See everything in perfect working order.

7. Say 'Thank you' for the fine work that your immune system does for you all day, every day.

8. Breathe in and open your eyes.

Chapter Six

And so, to sleep

We all need sleep. Six to eight hours of good quality sleep on average every night is considered ideal, but of course there are variables in nature, and as we are part of nature, not everyone conforms to the same rules. But, basically, the more sleep you get, or at least the better the quality of your sleep, the more mentally and physically proficient you will be during the day.

We spend around one third of our lives either sleeping or attempting to sleep, which if you are lucky enough to live until you are 90 years old, equates to approximately 30 years. Now that's a lot of Z's.

Why do we need to sleep?

Contrary to popular belief, our minds and bodies do not shut down while we are asleep. In fact, sleep is a very active period, where lots of processing, restoration and strengthening takes place. The body restores, rejuvenates, grows muscle, repairs tissue and manufactures hormones, while also organising and consolidating memories.

According to the latest figures, our brains take in 34 gigabytes of information every day. Every bit of this information needs to be processed and stored, and most of this happens while we sleep. Researchers have been studying the space between brain cells that increase during sleep, believing that this space allows for the brain to flush out toxins that build up during our waking hours. Now, I don't know about you, but my brain could definitely do with the occasional detox!

We sleep in cycles, usually totalling four-five per night. Each cycle typically lasts around 90 to 120 minutes, during which time the brain moves from slow-wave (non-REM) sleep to REM sleep, the dream state.

Stages of sleep

Stage one, the first stage of sleep, is known as light-stage sleep and lasts around five-ten minutes. During this stage, your mind and body begin to slow down, causing you to relax and feel drowsy. It is also the time when you can be woken easily.

Stage two is still considered light sleep, but now eye movement, brain waves and muscle activity decrease, preparing you for deeper sleep. It is believed that during this stage, most memories will be processed and stored.

Stages three and four are referred to as 'slow-wave sleep,' and are crucial to physical health, recovery and repair. The muscles of your body are fully relaxed in this stage, breathing slows down, blood pressure drops and body temperature decreases. You produce growth hormones, your immune system regulates and muscle tissue is repaired.

Stage Five is the period of REM (rapid eye movement) sleep, the dream state, and even though you are at the deepest level of sleep, there are a lot of neurological and physiological responses similar to being awake going on in this stage. Heart rate and blood pressure increase, and breathing can be irregular. Information and memories can now go from the short-term to the long-term memory.

Is there an art to getting a good night's sleep?

A good night's sleep is clearly fundamental to good health, so how can you get better at it? If you have difficulty falling asleep or staying asleep, there are lots of things you can do to regain your natural sleep pattern.

1. Limit, or better still, eliminate alcohol and stimulants like nicotine and caffeine in the evening. The effects of stimulants can last for several hours, so the chances of it affecting your sleep pattern are significant.

2. Try not to nap. Babies and children benefit from a daytime nap, but adults should try to

avoid nodding off during the day if sleeping at night is an issue. Establishing a regular sleep pattern that falls in line with darkness and light is key.

3. Try not to overeat or eat too late. If you eat late at night, your digestive system springs into action and prevents you from sleeping. Drinking too much fluid can overwhelm the bladder, resulting in frequent trips to the bathroom.

4. Create a comfortable sleeping environment. Temperature, lighting and noise should be controlled to make the bedroom conducive to falling (and staying) asleep.

5. Revise your bedtime activities. With the exception of the obvious bedtime activity, try not to do things that stimulate alertness, like scrolling through your phone, sending text messages, emails, reading news headlines, checking your bank balance or watching TV, all of which are things that stimulate brain activity.

6. Exercise. You knew this one would make an appearance on the list, right? It is true that our bodies are designed to be active during the day, but doing the right kind of exercise at the right time is also important. Studies have shown that cycling, for instance, enhances brain function more than running or jogging. The

time you exercise is also important. Many busy people can only find time to work out or participate in physical activity after work. Needless to say, cardiovascular exercise in the evening is not conducive to preparing the body for sleep, as even though your body may be exhausted, your brain has been stimulated.

7. Hypnosis. Self-hypnosis audio recordings are a wonderful way to prime the mind and body for sleep. We will cover this topic in more detail later in this book.

Sleep deprivation

Sleep deprivation has been used as a form of torture and a means of interrogation throughout history. It is now classified as one of five illegal interrogation techniques by the British military, alongside prolonged wall-standing, hooding, subjection to noise and food and drink deprivation. Sleep deprivation techniques are still used in the military, but not as a form of torture. Soldiers train exceptionally hard, and by exposing them to extreme fatigue during training, it demonstrates how it could affect their performance in combat, during tours of duty and in the event of capture and imprisonment.

Most of us will, at one time or another, experience exhaustion, irritability and a lack of focus due to a poor night's sleep, as any new parent or long-haul flyer will attest. Lack of sleep can affect your performance and your mood, and it can also lead to an increased risk of heart disease, as well as a greater likelihood of causing or being involved in an accident.

Sleep deprivation is something else altogether, though. To be deprived of sleep can result in speech impairment, hallucinations, paranoia and even psychosis.

Insomnia = the inability to sleep adequately

Many clients who come to see me for sleep problems usually begin by telling me that they are suffering with sleep deprivation. While they are indeed sleep-deprived, what they are actually experiencing is more likely to be insomnia. Insomnia can be acute or chronic, and it is usually the latter that causes problems. Some people have problems falling asleep, others staying asleep, and each one comes with their own set of challenges.

Trouble falling asleep can be caused by emotional issues such as worry, upset, stress, eating too late, jet lag, drinking too much coffee, alcohol or drug use. It can also be caused by physical issues, such as restless leg syndrome and breathing disorders.

Problems staying asleep occur for many reasons, including all of the above, and also nightmares, frequent trips to the toilet, dry mouth, hormone imbalances (e.g. menopause and prostate issues), a room that is too hot or too cold and has poor ventilation, too much noise or an uncomfortable bed.

I often have clients tell me that their parents remind them that they have always been a bad sleeper, or that their partners say they snore, sleepwalk, sleep talk or toss and turn all night. If you are told something often enough that you begin to believe it, it will inevitably become a reality for you. Your subconscious mind is not judging your thoughts or expectations, and so if you *know* that you will wake countless times during the night, or you *know* that you will fight to get to sleep, your subconscious mind will oblige, regardless. It will become a habit, and a habit is a learned behaviour.

I once heard the analogy that the thoughts we think as we drift off to sleep at night act as a marinade for the brain. I like that. Have you ever gone to sleep worrying about something, and then as soon as you wake up, the worry pops straight back in? Perhaps you have gone to bed angry, tossed and turned all night, and in the morning those angry feelings have come flooding back with a vengeance? So, if the thoughts you dwell on when you go to bed at night infuse your subconscious mind for the next six-eight hours, would it not be prudent to practise becoming consciously aware of your thoughts as you lie there? Reminding yourself of this analogy while you are about to go to sleep, with all the processing and storing of memories that this entails, is a powerful motivator for change.

You can choose your thoughts. That's right, you can *choose* your thoughts. When you become consciously aware of your thoughts, you can choose to change them, or you can choose to stew in them. I am not suggesting that you lie to yourself, or that you try to convince yourself of something you do not believe to be true. What I am suggesting is that you start to become aware of your pattern of thinking. Once you become more aware, you can instruct your subconscious mind that a solution to your problem / issue / dilemma will be worked on while you sleep, and that you will wake in the morning with clarity, answers, ways and means to overcome, to succeed or to move forward. This tactic is giving your subconscious mind a direct order; something positive to work on and marinate in while you allow your body to regenerate and your conscious mind to rest.

REM sleep boosts creativity. It connects new information to your existing database of information, and enables you to find answers to problems and come up with new ideas and inspiration while you sleep. The great inventor, Thomas Edison, would regularly take an afternoon nap in his armchair. As he prepared to rest, he would place a metal pan under the chair and hold some small metal balls in one hand. He knew that once he entered REM sleep, his body would become paralysed and thus he would drop the metal balls into the pan and immediately be woken up. He kept pen and paper by his chair, and as soon as he woke, he wrote down solutions to any problems that came to mind.

Is hypnosis deep sleep?

No, although it is easy to see why people perceive hypnosis as being a state of deep sleep, especially when many hypnotists still use the command 'Sleep!' when inducing a trance. The word 'Hypno' itself comes from the Greek 'Hypnos,' meaning sleep, and although hypnosis shares some of the same characteristics as sleep, it is certainly not a state of deep sleep. When you are in a hypnotic trance, your breathing becomes steadier and deeper, your heart rate slows, blood pressure drops, swallow reflex slows down and eyes flutter as the body and the mind relax. However, sleep is not a prerequisite, and if you were to drop off to sleep during a therapy session, a well-trained hypnotherapist would gently raise their tone or use your name to bring you back up to that blissful Theta state.

Dreams

Dreams can be entertaining, funny, sad, disturbing, frightening and downright bizarre.

We can dream anytime during the night, but our most vivid dreams are most notable during REM sleep. Studies have shown that dreams can have an effect on our health and wellbeing. Dr William Dement, of the Sleep Research Centre at Stanford University, discovered by waking participants just as they began to dream that they reported increased tension, anxiety and irritability, as well as difficulty concentrating, increased appetite, lack of coordination, feelings of emptiness and even hallucinations. The results of the study suggest that dreaming plays an important role in health and wellbeing, and that dream deprivation can have detrimental consequences.

Experts say that we dream between six-eight times each night. Even though we tend not to remember all of our dreams, we all dream. Legend has it that Paul McCartney composed the melody for Yesterday in a dream. He described the process of composing the song in *The Beatles Anthology*:

'I was living in a little flat at the top of a house and I had a piano by my bed. I woke up one morning with a tune in my head and I thought, *Hey, I don't know this tune -- or do I?* It was like a jazz melody... I went to the piano and found the chords to it, made sure I remembered it and then hawked it round to all my friends, asking what it was: "Do you know this? It's a good little tune, but I couldn't have written it because I dreamt it."'

According to psychoanalyst Carl Jung, dreams function on different levels, from telling us which parts of our psyche are out of balance to anticipating our future needs. Jung believed that our dreams are like stories, myths and archetypes, and that they are a valuable source of ideas and inspiration. Sigmund Freud (Jung's mentor) believed that our dreams represent repressed desires (primarily of the aggressive and sexual kind), and that they serve to help us sieve through unresolved issues or traumas.

For millennia, humans have pondered the cause and meaning of dreams, interpreting them, studying them, inducing them and even attempting to control them, as in 'lucid dreaming.' Ancient Egyptians believed that their Gods were revealed to them in their dreams, Ancient Roman literature is filled with accounts of dreams being prophecies and warnings, and Native Americans believe that dreams are a portal to otherworldly realms, and a means of communicating with ancestors and spirit guides. Dreams play an important role in many religions. Prominent biblical figures are said to have been visited by God and received important messages in their dreams.

People can train themselves to wake immediately following a dream, so that they can jot the dream down ready for analysis the following morning, and hundreds of books have been published over the years on the meaning and significance of dreams. Interpretations such as dreaming that your teeth are falling out infer that your life is falling apart, or if a man dreams about a baby, it means that his virility is lacking. Whatever your personal opinion is regarding dreams and their significance or insignificance – whether you believe they are flashes of inspiration, predictions of the future or just your brain unloading and processing things that are going on in your life – the whys and wherefores of dreaming and dreams remains a mystery.

Chapter Seven

Habits

'The chains of habit are too light to be felt until they are too heavy to be broken.'

– Bertrand Russell, British philosopher and author.

Habits can be useful. They automate routine activities, allowing you to reduce the number of sensory stimuli you might otherwise need, and thus freeing up your mind to concentrate on things that require more attention. As your subconscious mind does not discriminate or judge what is good or bad for you, anything that is repeated over time has the potential to become a habit. Repetition creates neural pathways. Simple. Your subconscious mind likes repetition. Your conscious mind, on the other hand, likes to learn new skills. It prefers logic and reasoning, and acts as a filter for your subconscious. Habits are a type of compulsion; they are behaviours that have developed over a period of time and have become automatic or unconscious actions.

Habits usually follow this pattern:

1. Trigger

2. Response

3. Reward

Example:

Trigger: Picking up your mobile phone.

Response: Check your social media posts

Reward: Lots of 'likes' / not enough 'likes.'

In this example, the reward can be positive or negative, so you either feel good or bad. Habits are like that.

Good habits are great. Walk into the bathroom, see your toothbrush and brush your teeth. Notice your gym shoes, put them on and go to the gym. Get into your car, check your surroundings and pull away safely.

Bad habits are not so good. See pack of cigarettes, light one up and inhale toxic fumes. Feel low, see a bottle of alcohol and drink too much. Cook for your children, notice their leftovers and, even though you're not hungry, eat said leftovers. Every time you act in a repetitive way, a specific neural pattern is stimulated, which ultimately becomes embedded in your brain.

The time it takes to create a new habit is debatable. If you search the internet, you will come up with anything from 21 days to 66 days to 254 days, but it really just boils down to how often the habit is performed and what the reward feels like. While both good and bad habits can make you feel good at the time, a bad habit can make you feel guilty, frustrated or angry with yourself for having fallen off the wagon or let yourself and others down.

Making or breaking a habit is not easy. Your brain is hardwired to take shortcuts and to do what comes most naturally, so while you are trying to reprogramme your subconscious mind to perform a new habit or break an old one, that same brain is busy working out how to revert back to your old ways. This is often referred to as 'the path of least resistance.'

We are not born with habits. Habits are formed; they have been practised and finely honed. They are patterns, behaviours and learned responses.

How to change bad habits into good ones

Exercise 6

Mr Motivator

1. Check your motivation monitor. You won't find it in the shops (yet), and it's totally free. It's a *feeling*. How motivated do you *feel* about changing a habit? Your success will be determined by your desire for change.

2. Begin with one habit at a time. Be clear on the habit you want to break and your reason for wanting to stop. Write it down.

3. Now, write down your triggers, including how you feel when you are *doing* the habit (e.g. feeling low, bored, etc.). Think about the times and *where* you are *when* you are most likely to carry out the habit.

4. Choose your new habit (preferably one with benefits!), and then write down your reasons for wanting to create this new behavioural pattern.

5. Set a time and date for the old habit to be broken. Write it down.

6. Share your news, preferably with people who will be supportive and who will not lure you back to your crafty old ways. By telling others about your good intentions, you are more likely to stick to them. After all, you do not want to have to admit to friends and family that you failed!

7. Practise.

8. Do not give up!

Remember that your subconscious mind likes repetition, and as Tony Robbins once said, 'Repetition is the mother of skill.'

My advice is to focus on establishing the new habit, rather than focussing on trying to stop the old one. Focussing on what you do not want is likely to create more of what you do not want. Ergo, focussing on what you want creates more of what you want!

Sometimes, a habit becomes so deeply ingrained that you may need to enlist the help of a professional therapist. If this is the case, hypnotherapy is a great choice. The reason why hypnotherapy works so well in helping to break bad habits is because it cuts through to the chase, working one-to-one with your subconscious mind, bypassing your critical mind and getting to the root of the behaviour. Once the root is discovered, you can detach from it, making room for the implementation of new and more beneficial behaviours.

Other modalities, such as cognitive behavioural therapy (CBT) and EFT tapping, are also great therapeutic tools to help break bad habits.

When a habit is more than a habit

Habits vs compulsive behaviour

Obsession is the thought; compulsion is the action.

OCD, or obsessive-compulsive disorder, is considered a mental illness and should be treated as such by experienced professionals. Someone with a compulsive disorder has no control over their behaviour, which can cause emotional distress and anxiety. People with compulsive disorders feel intense psychological pressure to repeat certain rituals in order to ease their anxiety and supress intrusive thoughts. OCD is fear-based; fear that something bad will happen if a particular routine or ritual is not performed; fear of being contaminated by germs, losing or not having the things they might need in a given situation. True OCD is unlikely to be overcome with positive thinking or the traditional habit-breaking methods outlined above. People with a diagnosis of OCD will need more complex treatment to address their condition.

In recent years, there have been a handful of celebrities and high-profile individuals who have declared themselves as being, 'a bit OCD.' The issue here is that while bringing mental health issues out into the open is a positive thing, it can also trivialise serious problems by making them appear trendy or quirky.

One of the most well-known OCD confessions came from Britain's own David Beckham, who spoke openly about his obsession with positioning a well-known brand of fizzy drink in his fridge. He is quoted as saying: 'I have got this obsessive-compulsive disorder, where I have to have everything in a straight line, or everything has to be in pairs. I'll put my Pepsi cans in the fridge, and if there's one too many then I'll put it in another cupboard somewhere.'

Goal, Pepsi!

Victoria Beckham apparently referred to her husband as a 'weirdo' due to his *eccentricities*. She speaks of them having three fridges: one for food, one for salad and another for drinks. David Beckham has also admitted to being *addicted* to tattoos. Although there are many reasons, both physical and psychological, why people like to have multiple tattoos, addiction not likely to be one of them. Addiction is defined as 'Not having control over doing, taking or using something to the point where it could be harmful to you.' (Source https://www.nhs.uk/live-well/healthy-body/addiction-what-is-it/)

Paul Hollywood, of *The Great British Bake Off*, confessed in the papers a few years ago that he, too, suffers with OCD, a condition that causes him to constantly clean his beloved Aston Martin, sometimes every few hours. Donald Trump dislikes shaking hands with people, and he has referred to himself as a 'germaphobe' who likes to wash his hands frequently and drink through a straw to avoid contamination. Now, it is perfectly acceptable to like the things in your life to be clean, tidy and organised; I am a fan of it myself. There is also nothing at all wrong with taking pride in your car, keeping your shelves well-stocked and avoiding potential health hazards, but are these examples truly OCD? I think not. There is an almighty chasm that lies between true OCD and perfectionism, and although perfectionism can occasionally present as a precursor to OCD, the two are most definitely not one and the same.

I have worked with clients who suffer with obsessive behavioural issues, addictions, trichotillomania (obsessive hair pulling), Asperger's, ADHD and autism, all of which can blur the lines and be confused with OCD. However, these are all separate conditions that need to be evaluated and treated accordingly.

In clinical hypnotherapy, we induce a state of deep relaxation to help ease the anxiety associated with the obsessive thoughts and urges. Clients learn to recognise the things that trigger their compulsions without identifying with or attaching emotion to them. Methods of treatment may include CBT, ego strengthening, regression therapy and exposure & response prevention (ERP). ERP is a type of CBT, or aversion technique, which involves gradually exposing a person to a feared object or obsession, such as dirt, and learning healthy ways in which to handle it effectively. There are many ways to treat and manage conditions such as these, and so a professional medical and psychological assessment is essential.

Cultivating good habits

So far, we have looked at habits – primarily bad ones – and how to change them from bad to better, and touched on how you may cultivate good ones. Now, let's delve a bit deeper and revisit Trigger, Response and Reward.

Think about something you do every day that makes you feel good. It could be something like going for a run, eating a hearty breakfast, reading a book in bed, settling down in the evening to watch a movie or cooking a meal for family or friends. Whatever you come up with, imagine doing that now, and then retrace the steps you take in order to carry it out.

If eating a hearty breakfast makes you feel good, what is the first step you take in preparation? The trigger could be a rumbling stomach, the response to gather the ingredients and the reward to sit down and enjoy, releasing all those *feel good* chemicals in the process.

I recall my son explaining the process he goes through most mornings prior to meditating. During the week, he wakes half an hour earlier than is necessary to get ready for work. He gets out of bed and has an almighty stretch *(this is his trigger)*. After the usual ablutions, he looks out of his window and begins deep abdominal breathing, which stimulates the release of endorphins *(the response)*. He meditates for 20 minutes or so, sets his intentions for the day or for the week, and then feels ready to take on the world armed with good vibes *(the reward)*.

And so, what new habit, behaviour or programme would you like to set up? Write it down on paper, a postcard or a post-it note and put it where you can see it; on your desk, your fridge, the bathroom mirror or anywhere else you will see it regularly. Keep it realistic and manage your expectations. It would be counter-productive to choose an unrealistic or unbelievable goal.

The key here is repetition. This is why so many religions encourage the daily reading of religious books, prayer and reciting affirmations. The more your read, re-read and repeat out loud, the stronger the message and the stronger your belief in your habits and, ultimately, how you live your life.

Chapter Eight

Willpower

***(The ability to resist short-term temptation
in order to meet long-term goals)***

'If only I had the willpower!'

'I have no self-control!'

'I can't help myself!'

'There's too much temptation out there!'

With more self-control, we would all very likely have healthier diets, take regular exercise, say no to drugs and alcohol, stop procrastinating and go on to achieve our goals and fulfil our dreams effortlessly. It is true to say that we all possess at least some willpower, and indeed use it occasionally to one extent or another, but the question is, why do some people seem to have more than others? Why can one person take a single biscuit while another has to eat the whole packet?

How much willpower you have and how long it lasts depends on many factors. Your mood, your beliefs, your health, your attitude, your levels of self-love and self-respect and how much of the precious reserve you spend! That's right. Research suggests that willpower is a finite resource, and so when you use it to resist lots of things at the same time, it simply burns out. An interesting fact is that exerting willpower burns glucose, and since glucose is the same fuel that powers your muscles, using too much willpower all at once can exhaust the body in the same way as a strenuous workout at the gym. But fear not, just like a muscle, exercising willpower gradually and persistently will strengthen your resolve.

Let's assume that you are trying to lose weight. You say 'No!' to temptation day and night, all week, perhaps even all month. You avoid sugary snacks, order a skinny latte instead of your usual caramel macchiato and you choose muesli and skimmed milk over a full English breakfast. You walk past the bakers with your head down, sure that a member of staff will recognise you and coax you inside; you say no to a drink after work or at the weekend, and generally steer clear of anything that smacks of weight gain. By now, though, your glucose levels have hit rock bottom; you need to replenish, and fast. At this point, you could fall off the proverbial wagon, have a binge and declare 'To hell with it!' Next day, you tell yourself that seeing as you have given into temptation, you may as well go back to your old pattern of eating, drinking and gaining weight. You have tried denying yourself, it failed to work, and so enough is enough, which leads us seamlessly on to the subject of deprivation.

When we deprive ourselves of the things that we enjoy or are accustomed to, we are more likely to lapse back into old habits and convince ourselves that after all the valiant effort, we deserve a treat. It is simply a case of finding balance, and with balance comes sustainability.

How to rev up willpower without the crash and burn

1. Becoming more self-aware is key to fostering willpower. Most of the choices we make are made automatically, without being consciously aware of what drives them and how they could affect our lives. Becoming more aware of the decisions you make, regardless how big or small, is a good start towards building willpower and resolve. Commit to keeping a daily or weekly log of all the choices you make, and at the end of the day or week, go over them and consider which choices supported your long-term goals and which ones did not. Remind yourself regularly of your goal and the reason you want to achieve it. Use images or write your goal somewhere you will see it every day.

2. Avoid perfectionism. If you are striving for perfection, you are more likely to set unrealistic goals, which in turn will make it

more likely that your willpower will wax and wane; you may wobble, stall or throw in the towel completely. A perfectionist is more likely to become disheartened if success persistently evades them, or if they receive criticism for not having the willpower to change. No one likes criticism, and no one less so than a perfectionist. Go easy on yourself. Set realistic goals that you know you can easily achieve.

3. Procrastination is the enemy. When attempting to build up reserves of precious willpower, putting decisions off is counterproductive. While you are busy making excuses for why you are not doing what you want or know you should be doing, you are setting the stage for frustration and disappointment. Again, set realistic goals, as most procrastination is based on the undertaking appearing too difficult or too daunting. Get rid of distractions, set a deadline and give yourself an incentive. Everyone likes to be rewarded, no matter how big or small. Just be sure that your reward does not fly in the face of that which you are willing!

4. Focus. I once read that the average human attention span is around eight seconds. This may explain why so many people fail to achieve their goals when relying on willpower alone; they simply lack focus. If you have ever sat on

your computer with a dozen tabs open or had a telephone conversation with the phone tucked under your ear, leaving your hands free to do other jobs, you were not focussed. Focus is fundamental to having and building willpower, not to mention supporting our health and wellbeing (why else would texting while driving be illegal?). You can clear away distractions and improve mental focus and concentration with meditation and mindfulness practise.

5. Hypnosis. If you want to train your brain to have more willpower, procrastinate less and focus more, you may need to go deeper. Ninety percent of everything you need to give up or build on lies inside the vault of your subconscious mind. Willpower requires thinking, which comes from your conscious mind, whereas your subconscious mind is your feeling mind. It triggers the reward centre of your brain and produces a dopamine rush when you experience the things you like. Be aware, however, that your subconscious mind can be a stubborn bedfellow. After all, you have practised the things that you want to give up for a while now, and they have become familiar programs.

Chapter Nine

Fears and phobias

*'For the thing I greatly feared has come upon me,
and what I dreaded has happened to me.'*
– Job, 3:25.

We are born with two fears: the fear of loud noises and the fear of being dropped. All other fears are learned responses.

Our primal instinct is to react to threatening and dangerous situations; this is in the interest of our survival. Without fear, we would not have lasted long as a race. Fear is felt in a part of the brain called the amygdala. The amygdala is responsible for our fight or flight response. It is also responsible for aggression, compassion, emotion and social interaction.

On 1 August 1966, a young man called Charles Whitman, who up until then had been a clever and popular student, climbed to the top of a tower at the University of Texas with a shotgun and began shooting into the crowd. He was eventually shot down, and at his autopsy it was discovered that he had a tumour in his brain that had been pressing on his amygdala. Although the initial autopsy was inconclusive regarding the role of the tumour in the shooting, a follow-up investigation by a group of scientists showed that it very likely played a part in the events of that day.

Researchers studying psychopaths and violent criminals have observed deformations of the amygdala, and they are looking now at the possibility of predicting potential criminals before a crime is committed, simply by measuring the amygdala. Science fiction perhaps, but how often has science fiction become reality? If you are of a certain age, you may remember the original *Star Trek* programmes, with Captain Kirk and crew using flip-up wireless phones to communicate, or Arnie Schwarzenegger as a passenger in a driverless car in *Total Recall*. I'm sure there are many other fine examples that could go towards proving a point here, too.

Thankfully, the vast majority of human beings on the planet possess a perfectly healthy amygdala. Not only does it play a vital role in the perception of emotions and the control of aggression, it also helps store memories so that we are able to recognise similar past events in the future. Your amygdala acts as an emotional thermostat, which you can turn up or down according to your anxiety levels. It is responsible for making snap decisions when it is appropriate to activate your fight or flight response. Your amygdala works on a subconscious level, and so does not discriminate between a real threat or a perceived one. It does not care if it is frightening you half to death with a *false positive* or a *false negative*. A false positive may be having the feeling that a ferocious dog sits behind a gate, but when the gate is opened, nothing is there. A false negative would be assuming there is no dog behind the gate when there actually is.

Your amygdala is concerned with trying to keep you safe and, based on past events (memories), it tries to protect you and not cost you dearly. We need our amygdala to monitor our fight, freeze or flight response, so that we stay safe and, hopefully, alive. This leads us nicely to the paradox of extreme sports and thrill seekers.

Base jumping, bungee jumping, free climbing, free diving, fast cars, motorbikes, mountaineering, swimming with sharks and so on. What is that all about? In a word, dopamine. Dopamine is your feel-good neurotransmitter, and when it is released, it feels wonderful! What happens when something feels so good? You do more of it.

How to increase dopamine without the aid of a wingsuit

Sleep hygiene: I am not talking about how and if you brush your teeth before bed, but a good sleep routine. Sleep fuels dopamine production.

Regular exercise: There is some exciting research going on right now around something called 'Blue Zones,' spearheaded by National Geographic Fellow, journalist and author, Dan Buettner. These are the five places in the world where people live the longest, healthiest lives. In Blue Zones, inhabitants do not go to the gym, pump iron or sweat it out in aerobic classes; they get up and move every 20 minutes or so as a matter of course, which to my way of thinking is the epitome of *regular* exercise. More information can be found at https://www.bluezones.com

Healthy diet: Here it is again, but you really are what you eat. A diet rich in tyrosine may be useful, as this amino acid is thought to increase levels of the neurotransmitters dopamine, adrenaline and noradrenaline, which may help improve memory and performance in stressful situations. The word 'tyrosine' comes from the Greek *tyrós*, meaning cheese, and not only is it found in some cheeses, but also in almonds, bananas, avocados, eggs, beans, fish and chicken.

Stress avoidance: Our stress response reduces the neurotransmitters previously mentioned, and so try using techniques such as meditation, visualisation, hypnosis, massage, walking outdoors, walking your dog, stroking your cat, socialising, breathing exercises and so on, to reduce stress and release a healthy dose of dopamine.

When a fear is more than just a fear

Most fears are rational. When a fear is irrational, it is referred to as a phobia.

A phobic response is when someone has an exaggerated or unrealistic fear response to a certain situation or object. More often than not, the symptoms are felt when a person comes into direct contact with the situation or object, but for some, the symptoms can be brought on simply by thinking about it.

Phobias are generally broken down into two categories: specific phobias and complex phobias.

Specific phobias, or 'simple phobias,' usually centre on a specific object, situation or activity, and develop at a young age. These tend to be things like fear of spiders, snakes, dogs, open water, injections, visiting the dentist and so on, and do not usually interfere with everyday life.

Complex phobias, on the other hand, can severely affect a person's quality of life. This type of phobia tends to develop in adulthood and stems from a deep-rooted anxiety around a certain situation or circumstance. Two of the most common complex phobias are agoraphobia (the fear of open spaces) and social phobia (fear of social situations).

Phobias work on a subconscious level; they are learned behaviours which make them particularly responsive to hypnotherapy. In hypnotherapy, you can unlearn the fear response, build up your exposure to the phobia and in time ease the associated anxiety.

A note on panic or anxiety attacks

These bursts of intense fear can come on suddenly and regularly, and for no apparent reason. Symptoms can be as diverse as sweating, trembling, shortness of breath, chest pain, nausea, dizziness, a racing heart, fear that you are losing your mind or that you could actually die.

Typically, the first port of call for people who suffer with anxiety attacks will be antidepressants, opioids or beta-blockers, thus treating it much like depression. Today, we are seeing more health and medical practitioners recommending alternative therapies, such as clinical hypnotherapy, EFT (emotional freedom technique), EMDR (eye movement desensitisation and reprocessing), CBT and CBH as replacements for addictive pharmaceuticals.

A note on depression

While I am not devoting an entire chapter to the subject of depression in this book, I would like to address it, as I see it in my clinic all too often. Depression is more than simply feeling unhappy or fed up for a few days.

Most of us will, at one time or another, go through periods of feeling a bit low, but depression is a *deep* sadness felt persistently over a much longer period of time, and is not something you can easily 'snap out' of. Depression is an illness. Depression can be mild, moderate or severe, and those with severe depression can feel hopeless and are likely to suffer with low self-esteem, lethargy, problems sleeping, eating, socialising and functioning in general.

What causes depression?

Often, there will be a trigger. It could be bereavement, losing your job, financial hardship, separating or divorcing, prolonged illness or even having a baby. Some say that you are more likely to suffer with depression if you have a family history of it, but you can also become depressed for no apparent reason.

What can you do about it?

Prescribed medication certainly has its place in the treatment of depression. However, therapies such as clinical hypnosis, EFT, EMDR, CBT, CBH and counselling, as well as behavioural strategies like goal setting, taking up a hobby, keeping a journal or diary-highlighting positive things that have happened during your day could all help lift your mood. Avoid sitting or lounging around for long periods of time, keep busy and consume foods rich in dopamine-producing chemicals.

Medical disclaimer

This article is intended for information purposes only, and not as medical advice. Those seeking medical advice regarding the diagnosis and treatment of depression should consult with their primary care provider and / or pharmacist.

Chapter Ten

The human condition

Have you ever had a gut feeling? Something deep inside of you – a voice, a nudge or an inner knowing? Would it surprise you to know that you have neurons in your gut? There are millions of neurons in your intestinal nervous system. These nerve cells help you to feel things. Whether you call it instinct or intuition, everyone experiences it from time to time, and what may be even more interesting to learn is that you can harness these gut instincts. Science tells us that 90 percent of the fibres in our vagus nerve transmit information from the gut to the brain, not the other way around.

We humans have many attributes that non-humans do not possess, with doubt being one of them. There are two types of doubt:

1. Self-doubt, which can present as a lack of confidence or low self-esteem

2. The kind of doubt whereby we suspend belief or judgement and start asking questions

Asking questions involves active listening. When you are actively listening, you are taking time to process information and allowing your conscious mind to decode it and see if it fits with your beliefs. Whether it's self-belief, religious belief, blind faith or a belief that something other than yourself exists, your belief system can help or hinder you. You can be rigid in a belief that keeps you standing still and afraid to branch out, preventing you from being the best you can be or to do the things you long to do. Belief can also keep you safe, e.g. believing, or rather trusting, your gut to let you know when you are in danger, or when something just does not feel right.

On 6 May 1953, a young Roger Bannister had an unwavering belief. He believed that he could run a mile faster than anyone had ever done before. Up until that time, people thought that it was impossible for the human body to run too fast, and that it would simply collapse under the pressure. However, Bannister was able to create a certainty within himself without any proof that it could be done. Was it blind faith, self-belief or gut feeling? Whatever the case, as soon as there was *evidence* that a mile could be ran in four minutes, others had a go, and now over 1,400 athletes have either matched or broken Bannister's record.

Most of us will challenge or doubt our intuition more often than trust it. We apply reason and logic to decisions, doubt our choices and throw in a few convincing examples based on past experiences or negative hearsay, to find evidence for not doing or trying what we really want. We stay put and often stuck, so that we do not fail or embarrass ourselves. Then, there are those who throw caution to the wind, trust their gut with unwavering belief and come up smelling of roses. What makes us all so different?

Most of our thoughts, choices and decisions are based on previous experiences; we predict future events based on past events. Now, while that is certainly prudent when it comes to having experienced the pain of putting ones finger on a naked flame or jumping off the shed roof with an umbrella, pretending to be Mary Poppins, and fracturing your ankle (or was that just me?), it can also prevent us from listening and nurturing the brain in our gut.

The feeling you get in your gut can easily be misinterpreted. You can get butterflies when you are excited or joyful, but then get the same *feeling* when you are nervous or afraid. How to tell the difference? That is the key.

There are times where you will be blissfully unaware of your intuition until you get a nudge, which could be thought of as a coincidence or a series of seemingly unrelated events. The nudges, signs or signals eventually come together like pieces from a jigsaw, and suddenly the bigger picture is staring you in the face. This is called synchronicity, and it is more than just coincidence.

A coincidence is something that occurs by luck or chance, like bumping into an old friend in the middle of a crowded city, whereas synchronicity is deeper and more meaningful. Synchronicity is a nudge or a pull towards something, coming from a deeper intelligence, the universe, God, inner voice or whatever you choose to call it. It is when a sequence of seemingly unrelated events draws you to where you need to be or what you should be doing at a particular time and place.

A little over 20 years ago, I was determined to start a new life for myself and my children. Having recently come out of an unhappy relationship, I was feeling inspired, confident and ready to take on a new challenge. My dream was to start a business that would enable my children and I to live in the Caribbean (I am a big dreamer), and to be fair, I was halfway towards that very goal when everything ground to a halt. Everything I had built started falling apart, and every which way I turned, I hit another metaphorical brick wall. My dream bubble burst, and in its place lay a muddy puddle. With heavy heart, I accepted defeat (most unlike me), as well as a highly demanding job back in London.

Before I could take up the new role, I had to attend a training course at a hotel that was miles from home, along one of the most notoriously awful motorways in the South East of England. As luck would have it, one of the perks of the job was a company car, which I hoped would make the journey much more tolerable. On my first day, I met with the fleet manager, who ushered me through a never-ending row of shiny new Mercedes. My heart leaped and I was ready to land, but as we neared the end of the row, he clicked the key fob he had been enticing me with and handed over the keys to a three-year-old Ford Sierra. My heart sank; the landing was a flop, but despite the disappointment, I soldiered on.

On the rainy and congested drive up to the hotel and conference centre, the radio gave up the ghost and left me with no other station than one which happened to be playing Elton John classics from the 1970s. Fearing that the week would continue along the same vein, I threw caution to the wind and rain and began to sing along to Daniel, a song that would prove an annoying earworm for days after. On the course, I teamed up with a colleague who had become insistent that he had a friend I simply had to meet. I politely declined on numerous occasions, since I was there to work, not meet the man of my broken dreams, and certainly not someone chosen by someone I hardly knew. One evening after dinner, my self-proclaimed cupid announced that his friend would be driving down from London to join us for drinks.

'Oh, that's just perfect,' I scowled, rolling my eyes and ordering another G&T

His friend arrived as promised, and as he joined us, he stumbled and dropped his car keys on the floor; the keys to a *Mercedes*. It turned out that his name was *Daniel*, and he was tall, dark, handsome and of

Caribbean descent. Today, Daniel is my husband, my soul mate and my best friend, and we have been together for over 22 years. Coincidence or synchronicity?

My personal take on synchronistic events is that they are signposts guiding and directing us, helping us to align with a higher intelligence to assist us in our personal growth. Take a moment or two to think of any synchronicities that have happened to you on your journey so far. Have you acted on them or let them pass by?

Your inner critic

As well as having gut feelings, we also have an inner critic, which is that annoying voice that tells you such things as, 'You are not good enough / clever enough / pretty enough / handsome enough / educated enough...' It's the irritating voice that kindly reminds you of what happened the last time you tried something different, spoke up or stepped out of your comfort zone.

Your inner critic lives in a perpetual state of fear. Fear of failure or of not ever being good enough; fear of humiliation or of ruin, or of being exposed as an imposter.

(NB: I recently read a wonderfully insightful book on this subject, The Chimp Paradox, by Professor Steve Peters. A highly recommended read.)

Imposter syndrome

Imposter syndrome is a feeling of inadequacy and incompetence, despite all the evidence that points to you being highly skilled or knowledgeable in your field. Regardless of status, anyone can suffer from imposter syndrome, but it is particularly noticeable in perfectionists and those who set their bar very high.

Great Britain's heptathlon gold medallist Karina Johnson-Thompson admitted to experiencing imposter syndrome after winning her medal at the 2019 World Championships. Neurosurgeons and high-ranking physicians, who shoulder monumental responsibility for their patients and their outcomes, doubt themselves from time to time, wondering how and why they have become so good at what they do and if it will last.

Speaking in London a few years ago, Michelle Obama spoke about how she had felt out of place throughout her life. 'I had to overcome the question, "am I good enough?"' she said. 'It's dogged me for most of my life. Many women and young girls walk around with that question in their minds.' She went on to say, 'It's sort of like, "you're actually listening to me?" It doesn't go away, that feeling of "I don't know if the world should take me seriously. I'm just Michelle Robinson, that little girl on the south side who went to public school."'

Yours truly has suffered with the malaise of imposter syndrome. Many of my clients are referred to me by medical professionals, or by gracious word-of-mouth recommendations from clients who have turned their lives around after having worked with me, and there are times where I look back at the journey that has led me to where I am today and ask, *How did I get here? Do I know enough? Should I know more?*

There is also a condition known as a God complex. I call it a condition, as it is a state of mind that can manifest into form. By this, I do not mean literally turning into a God, but rather thinking that you are bestowed with God-like abilities. You may recognise it in people who have an over-inflated sense of self-importance or entitlement, and who require constant admiration; people who think they are always right, beyond reproach, above the law and never to blame. You could call it narcissism or egomania. These individuals could be heads of state, celebrities, surgeons, lawyers, billionaires or criminals who believe they are above mere mortals. Thankfully, God complex is a psychological illusion.

The inner you, however, is what we are looking at here.

Divine energy, spiritual energy, your inner soul, your essence, source energy or universal energy... call it what you will, but *who* or *what* looks out from behind your eyes? Think about it. When you look in the mirror, you see a face with all its unique features gazing back at you. You may spend a little time finding fault here and there, picking, poking, pulling and checking your teeth for spinach, or debating whether or not you need to shave, apply makeup or style your hair, but how much time, if any, do you spend seeing YOU? Would you think it madness to have a conversation with yourself in the mirror? A simple 'Good morning' or 'How are *we* feeling today?' Despite the old saying that talking to yourself is the first sign of madness, quite the opposite is true. In fact, checking in with yourself regularly, if not daily, is in my humble opinion nothing short of genius.

Exercise 7

Are we OK?

'Mirror, mirror, on the wall, who's the fairest of them all?' – Mantra of the Evil Queen, *Snow White and the Seven Dwarfs*.

(Tools required: 1x mirror)

1. Take a good look. Get any picking, poking, preening, put downs or self-adulation out of the way and take a deeper look. Remove

judgement. This is not an exercise in critique or a time for analysis. See yourself with empathy, not judgement. No one knows you like you know you, and no one sees you like you see you – fact!

2. What is it that you would like other people to know about you? What do you see beneath your exterior that you would like others to see?

3. Go on, say it. You are talking to yourself about yourself in total privacy, so remind yourself of all the good and marvellous things you know to be true about YOU. If you feel a bit silly and want to laugh, LAUGH!

4. Ask yourself, 'Are we OK?' Regardless of whether the answer is yes or no, strike up a conversation. Go ahead, talk to yourself. It's perfectly normal, and surprisingly good for your mental and emotional health.

If you notice any negative thoughts creeping into your mind, don't break the mirror like the Evil Queen did, but challenge them. You are more handsome/ beautiful in person than you are in the mirror. Real beauty is not exterior, but emanates from within.

Chapter Eleven

Meditation

'Oh, I can't meditate.'

'I can't switch off.'

'I don't have the time.'

'I can't stop thinking.'

Anyone and everyone can meditate. Everyone can switch off, or rather, turn the volume down a tad. Everyone can find a few minutes in the day where there's no need to worry about thinking. Besides, meditation does not require you to stop thinking, because in truth we can never *really* stop. Even when we are deeply asleep, our thoughts are still going on in the background; we are just not aware of them.

If time is a serious problem for you, why not try mediating in bed, on the sofa, in an armchair, in a tent or wherever it is that you slumber. Go to your place of sleep BEFORE you become too sleepy or exhausted, so that you can experience the wonderful meditative state before slipping off into dreamland. It is not obligatory to adopt 'the pose' (albeit it's preferable) in order to meditate. You can meditate sitting on a chair or lying in bed. Just get comfortable and become still.

Meditation is a technique used for resting the mind and achieving a state of consciousness different to your normal waking state. The word 'meditation' stems from the Latin *meditatum*, 'to ponder.' But not everyone agrees on where the practise of meditation originated. You would be forgiven for assuming it originated with Buddha, as I once did, but the origin of meditation is still debated.

The Tibetan word for meditation is *gom*, which translates as 'become familiar with,' and I for one quite like that definition. Becoming familiar with oneself and getting to know yourself, warts and all; sitting still with yourself. It can be a little disconcerting, uncomfortable and possibly intimidating at first, but it is an essential component of discovering, and therefore being able to become, all you can possibly be.

In the following exercise, I will attempt to communicate my own personal way of getting into a meditative state. Feel free to follow it to the letter, or to adapt it until you find your own way. I usually wake up an hour earlier than is necessary, or sometimes only half an hour, but always enough so that I'm not rushed. It is highly unlikely that you will be able to meditate when you are focussing on the time.

Devices (of the non-computer type) have been used to measure and keep track of time for thousands of years. From sundials to hourglasses and pendulums to mechanical clocks, we humans have always been fixated with time. I rarely use an alarm clock, and unless I have an early flight to catch, I rely on my internal body clock, which has rarely (if ever) let me down. I set an intention to wake around a certain time, and each time, I wake with minutes to spare. This is not magic, nor is it particularly clever. We all possess a body clock. Our biological clock is controlled by the part of our brain called the suprachiasmatic nucleus, or the SCN. This group of time-telling cells are located in the hypothalamus, and they respond to signals of light and dark. And so, in the mornings, when we are exposed to light, the SCN sends a signal to raise body temperature and produce hormones like cortisol. Your SCN also responds to light by delaying the release of other hormones, such as melatonin. Melatonin is produced when the eyes signal to the SCN that it is dark, thus promoting sleep. It is little wonder that melatonin, and therefore sleep quality, has become a victim of the dreaded blue light effect (the blue light that is emitted from computer screens can delay the release of melatonin, increase alertness, and reset the body's internal clock to a later schedule).

I digress, and so back to meditation. Meditation is not sleep. Your aim during meditation is really just to become still. At first, you may only manage a few minutes, and this is fine. It takes practise, and as my mother used to say, 'Practise makes... perfect.' A lovely thought though it is, Mother, perfection is something

I have long since stopped striving for, as anyone who has ever seen the interior of my fridge at home will attest (**Note to self:** never invite the Beckhams over for drinks).

People often get frustrated while trying to sit still and quiet the mind. Remember, your mind is never quiet while you are awake, and so rather than focus on thoughts, just allow your thoughts to drift and to pass through your mind like thought bubbles or clouds. I love a certain quote from the Zen monk, Shunryu Suzuki, and I always think of it whenever my thoughts become too intrusive or too loud:

'Leave your front door and your back door open. Allow your thoughts to come and go. Just don't serve them tea.'

My personal preference is to meditate for 20 minutes first thing in the morning, ideally to music or 'soundwaves,' aka binaural beats. 'Binaural' means 'relating to both ears,' and so for optimal impact, I listen to these tones through headphones. The premise is that your left ear receives a 300-hertz tone and your right ear receives a 280-hertz tone, resulting in your brain absorbing a 10-hertz tone (science can be precise, but also finicky). Cocooned in relaxing music, these subtle beats pulsate deep inside the brain, so you do not even need to notice the sounds for your brain to be affected by them (studies have shown that when you listen to low-frequency tones, brainwave activity slows down). Needless to say, when your brainwave activity slows down, it is easier for you to relax, making it easier for you to get into a meditative state. There is a lot of research on the subject of binaural beats, and I encourage you to make your own decision as to whether or not it enhances your meditation practise.

A few years ago, the pharmaceutical company Bayer, who manufacture ©Aspirin, added seven downloadable files of binaural beats to its Austrian website. The idea that the beats induce a state of calm, which in turn could help alleviate headaches, is what inspired the move. You can probably still find the files here: https://www.aspirin.at/good-vibes/wie-funktionieren-binaurale-beats/

(NB: despite everything I believe in, practise, teach and have taught over the years, it was my own son who introduced me to the joy of daily meditation. My children continue to lift and inspire me every day.)

Exercise 8

Quiet time

1. Make yourself comfortable, preferably in a place where you are unlikely to be disturbed. Close your eyes.

2. Breathe into your abdomen, breathing in deeply through your nose and slowly out through your mouth. As you breathe in, imagine breathing in a sense of calm. You might imagine calm as a colour or a shape, or perhaps just sense it; there is no right or wrong way. As you breathe out, allow your lips to part without pursing or shaping them.

3. Imagine your breath is a breeze that blows away any unhelpful or intrusive thoughts. Imagine your mind as a beautiful big room, and you are throwing the windows and doors of your mind open to let your thoughts blow out and drift far away, like having a spring clean. Starting at the top of your head, scan your body, noticing any areas of tension, and breathe tension out through the windows and doors of your mind. If you need to adjust your position, do so. As you become more comfortable, you will begin to notice your thoughts drifting. Do as Shunryu Suzuki suggests and allow them in, but do not offer them an incentive to stay. Every time your thoughts drift, bring your focus back to your breath.

4. Now, open your heart. Think of someone, something or some place that you love deeply. Be very present in the moment. Absorb any and all of the sensations, the feeling of love. See

what you see, hear what you hear. Embrace all of it. Breathe in deeply.

5. Now is the moment to set your intention for the day (or for the following day, if you are mediating in the evening). Enjoy the moment. Do not try to stop thinking. Just allow and breathe. As you continue to relax and breathe deeply, your brain begins to secrete those happy chemicals. Soak them up.

6. Stay in this moment for as long as feels right.

7. Open your eyes whenever you feel ready. You may be surprised at how long you have been in meditation.

Setting your intention

Your intention could be something as simple as telling yourself you will have a good day, or that you will smile at someone or be kind to yourself. It may be to have a successful meeting or to not shout at your children, partner or spouse. It may be to achieve something big or small during the day, to promote healing in your body or your mind, or to feel inspired or motivated. This morning, before I sat down to write, I set the intention to finish this chapter before I left the house. I visualised my fingers tapping away and the words flowing through me, effortlessly, onto the screen of my laptop. Intention accompanied by visualisation anchors it in your subconscious mind, and it is therefore considered a done deal.

Visualisation

People often tell me they cannot visualise because they are not creative or their mind 'just isn't wired that way.' If you are part of the group who believe you cannot use your creative mind to visualise, I invite you to test your theory.

Caveat 1: in 2015, scientists described a condition known as aphantasia, acknowledging that there are some people who are unable to visualise mental images. The condition is rare, and so unless you have been diagnosed with this condition, you will be able to visualise.

Caveat 2: blind / sight impaired people who are born blind do not visualise in the same way as those with sight. However, with the brain being completely adaptable, it has been suggested that blind people instead visualise by touch, smell, temperature and memory. People who lose their sight during their lives will most likely continue to visualise in images.

If you have sight, you are visually wired. Ninety percent of the information transmitted to your brain will be taken in visually, and these images will be processed 60,000x faster than the written word.

Bonus exercise

Close your eyes and take a few deep breaths. Imagine you are walking along a pristine white, sandy beach. Notice how the sand feels under your feet and between your toes. Listen to the sound of the ocean waves as they crash onto the shore; see the white froth of the waves as they land. Inhale the salty sea air. Stand still and look out onto the horizon. When you look out onto a clear horizon, you see how the ocean meets the sky, and you can get a real sense of being on and being part of this beautiful planet. Breathe in deeply.

Open your eyes.

Chapter Twelve

Mindfulness

'Wherever you go, there you are.'

Mindfulness is defined as: 'The psychological process of purposely bringing one's attention to experiences occurring in the present moment without judgment.' (Source: Wikipedia.)

Mindfulness is nothing new. It has been around for centuries. It is ancient and spiritual, and much like government taxation laws, it gets a revamped name every now and again, but the fundamentals remain unchanged.

Mindfulness today is a multi-billion-dollar business, and if the research is correct, it works. The National Institute for Clinical Excellence (NICE) endorses it as a beneficial treatment for depression, and some 30 percent of British GPs now refer their patients for mindfulness-based treatment. Clinical hypnotherapy is a mindfulness-based treatment. Indeed, hypnotherapy for issues such as IBS, depression, smoking cessation and birthing is endorsed by NICE. The British Medical Journal (BMJ) recommend hypnotherapy for depression, anxiety and pain management.

Mindfulness programmes are being taught to teachers and employers in order that they be implemented in schools and workplaces. You can find mindfulness experiences offered at health spas, pop-up and drop-in venues and mother and toddler groups, and there are even mindful workouts conducted at gyms.

So, what could be driving this surge in popularity? The likely answer is a rise in stress and depression worldwide. As such, mindfulness is big business, offering a low-cost, drug-free, organic solution with zero negative side effects. More recently, there has been an 'appification' of mindfulness. The internet is currently awash with mindfulness apps, offering anything from three-minute to 30-minute *moments* to unwind.

Technology is a wonderful thing, essential to how we live our lives today, but it also has a darker side. More and more people, especially younger generations, are suffering from stress and anxiety due to time spent looking at a blue screen rather than interacting with real people in real time. Social media, cyber bullies, trolls, photoshopped pictures showcasing unrealistic body images and false lifestyles are all fodder used to further confuse young minds. Is it not slightly ironic that we are using apps to help us disconnect from the stresses of technology? Analysis suggests that most people give up on these apps within a couple of weeks of downloading them, raising questions about how useful a techno quick-fix really is. Nevertheless, used wisely, mindfulness is a wonderful practise that can change how you perceive everything in and around you. In the best possible way, of course.

Is mindfulness the same as meditation?

Mindfulness differs from meditation in that mindfulness focusses on *something*, e.g. your body, whereas meditation focusses on *no-thing*. When you are being mindful, your awareness is heightened, but when you are meditating, you go beyond the mind and the body into a peaceful bliss.

Is it hypnosis?

Not really, although as I mentioned, hypnosis has elements of mindfulness. The difference here is that hypnosis involves being responsive to suggestion. It is a goal-driven therapy, and while being focussed on the body and thoughts is conducive to settling into a therapy session, awareness is gradually toned down in order to focus on specific thoughts, sensations or behaviours in order to facilitate positive change.

Mindfulness is about being in the present moment, connecting to what is going on inside and outside yourself moment by moment, and then becoming aware of your body and the sensations it experiences using all five senses.

Exercise 9

Munching mindfully

(Tools required: 1x moreish morsel)

Go and grab something to eat; just a small something, like a piece of fruit, a square of chocolate, a biscuit, a vegetable or anything else that takes your fancy. Look at it in your hand. Start to observe it, turn it over and around; notice the colour, size, shape, temperature and weight; notice everything about it. Whatever foodstuff it is, put it to your nose and smell it. Notice if you begin to salivate. Now, put it in your mouth or take a bite, holding it there for a moment. Notice how your tongue feels as it comes into contact; notice your taste buds spring to life and your sense of smell turning up a notch. Start to chew or suck. Notice the sounds you make; the sounds and the sensation of the food under the pressure of your teeth, your tongue and the roof of your mouth. Become aware of your jaw as it moves up and down and back and forth, preparing the food for swallowing and digestion. Think about the enzymes in your saliva, and notice how they begin to work on breaking the food down. Chew or suck slowly and savour the taste, textures and aromas. Swallow when you are ready. Congratulations, you have just practised mindfulness.

Back in the Victorian era, there was a fad where people would chew each mouthful of food fifty times. Aptly named the 'Chew-Chew' diet, the Victorians used it as a way of losing weight without the inconvenience of actually dieting. All foods were allowed as long as each mouthful was chewed 50 times, the logic being that the longer you took to chew, the less food you would eat. What they were actually doing was practising mindful eating.

How to bring mindfulness into your everyday life and reap the benefits

Think for a moment about the last exercise. Aside from the fact that by chewing your food thoroughly, you are starting the digestive process before food hits your stomach, thus making things easier on your digestive system, you are also connecting with the physical and emotional act of eating; of fuelling and nourishing your body. So, rather than stuffing a sandwich down in 30 seconds flat during your lunch hour or chomping on an apple as you run from the house, you engage in the process. You will start to appreciate the look of your food, how it is presented, the textures and flavours – sweet, sour, salty, bitter or savoury – and be able to detect most every ingredient that has gone into creating the dish. You may even become gastronomic!

By practising mindful eating, you will naturally move on to noticing other things that you do and usually take for granted. So many of us live our lives at an incredible pace. Days, weeks, months and years fly by at such speed, we miss much of what is going on around us. Seeing as we only get one shot at this life (apparently), we surely do ourselves an injustice by not engaging fully in it. Not all moments will be wonderful, that is true, but even during less fortunate times, there may be lessons to learn, things you can teach others and experiences to be had creating memories, ideas, inspiration or motivation.

Imagine that instead of rushing to work, running for the bus or train or dashing through a school run, you were to become more mindful. Step out of your front door and take a few seconds to look up at the sky and really appreciate it. Enjoy the air you are breathing (even if you live in the city), the buildings, the trees, the grass, the houses, the people, the cars, the bikes, the streets and everything that runs beneath. Take more time to listen to what is being said, and to consider your words before you speak them. Now, I am well aware this may sound as though I think we should be pretending that we live in a town called Pleasantville – I am a realist, after all – so, what I am suggesting is that it may be interesting to bring mindfulness into some of the everyday things you do. Use moments here and there to really notice what surrounds you; the people, places and the things you share your existence with on our lovely blue planet.

I wonder how many days are lost just trying to get through them. I hear it said a lot – 'I'm just trying to get through the day!' – and given what little time each of us has on this planet, what better time to change than now. Even when days get tough, try to be more present. Being more present will help guide you through the day, like a GPS system helping you to avoid potential roadblocks and sharp bends in the road ahead.

What have you got to lose? Time? Time is constantly ticking by. Time can never be replaced.

Every moment matters.

Chapter Thirteen

Superheroes and superpowers

Thanks to comic books and moviemakers, superheroes with superhuman superpowers are familiar to us all. It is fun to see them in action, fighting crime and living their best life with their miraculous powers. I imagine most of us have, at one time or another, wished to have been born with a superpower, but sadly, these are fictional characters with imaginary powers bestowed upon them by the minds of ordinary humans. But then again, there have been plenty of documented cases about people with extraordinary abilities; some are born with these abilities, while others have achieved them with dedication and practise.

Take Wim Hof, for example. Wim has been dubbed 'the Iceman,' after he discovered that by controlling his breath, he could withstand freezing temperatures that would ordinarily kill a human in a matter of minutes. David Blaine, the street magician, pushes himself to feats of endurance that most mere mortals could not sustain. Isao Machii, the Japanese martial artist, possesses reflexes so fast, he can slice a bullet in half with a sword as it is fired towards him. There are people with extraordinary memory recall, remarkable strength and IQs that are off the scale, and individuals with heightened senses, as in synaesthesia, the ability to 'see' words and 'hear' sounds as colours. So, is it possible that we could all possess a superhuman ability or two?

I say yes, depending on your point of view, of course. How about when you are in *the zone* or in *the flow*? Athletes, artists, musicians and entrepreneurs, like Bill Gates and Richard Branson, accomplish tremendous things while in this coveted state. In positive psychology, the flow state, or being in the zone, is the mental state of a person performing an activity with complete focus and absorption, to the extent that they lose sense of space and time.

Discovering your superpower

Unlike my own childhood endeavour of taking to the sky with a black umbrella and carpet bag, like Mary Poppins, discovering that you possess a real superpower would be utterly life-changing, would it not? Now, the creation of most superheroes usually begins with them having had a sad beginning or experience: a loss, an accident or a darkness. These heroes begin a quest for meaning and purpose, and eventually discover the powers within.

Your superpower is your unique talent; your USP, so to speak. Unfortunately, many of us are unaware of our unique talent, our abilities and our strengths, often because we doubt ourselves or feel pressured to conform to other people's ideas of who and what we should be. So, how can you find yours?

Start by finding out what makes you tick, what makes you feel wonderful and what brings out your passion. For me, I love everything to do with the human mind; I love to work with people and help them to achieve and exceed their goals and live their best lives. I am blessed in that I enjoy going to work every single day. However, when I am writing, I am in a state of bliss; I lose all perception of time and only get up from my desk when my backside has gone numb. On a day when my plan is that I will do nothing but write, I wake up feeling excited and infused with inspiration. My superpower, that is the thing that energises me physically and emotionally, is writing.

One of our grandsons, as another example, plays football. Really, though, this is an understatement. He lives and breathes football, and this has been the case since he could walk. In fact, chasing after a football is probably what prompted him to walk in the first place. Football is his passion. He cries if he can't play; he would play all day, every day from dawn until dusk if he could. At the time of writing, he is almost eight years old and has already been offered contracts by three Premier League football teams. This is his superpower, and he has been blessed to discover it early and naturally. With the continued support of the family, I am in no doubt that he will use his superpower to become a superstar and go on to live his dream.

Dreams vs reality

I will be the first to admit that there is much about the planet, the universe and technology I do not fully understand. For instance, how it is I can take a picture on my phone, send it to my son in Singapore, have him receive it, be alerted to the fact that he has actually looked at it, and then have him reply in a matter of seconds? To be honest, I do not give it that much thought; I just enjoy doing it. I do not really understand how electricity works, but I do not really question it, I just use it, and the same goes for quantum physics. What I will attempt to do, however, is put in layman's terms what I think quantum physics is about.

Let's say, for example, you wake up one morning, and instead of going through your normal routine, you make the decision to do something altogether different. You leap out of bed, your mind starts to race with ideas and possibilities, and adrenaline surges though your body as excitement grows. You find yourself faced with hundreds of decisions that must now be made. You could change anything or do anything; you could skip breakfast, go outside in your underwear, do a hundred star jumps, sing a chorus of *Halleluiah*, purchase a one way ticket to Honolulu, buy a lama and trot off to join a monastery in Peru... or you could snuggle back down under the covers and try again tomorrow. You see, quantum physics is about infinite possibility.

So, now let's assume you decide to tuck back in under the duvet. All the other possibilities you imagined are now unreal; they are not part of your reality, but they might have been. You could potentially have done any of those things if you really wanted to. What you *do* becomes your reality, while what you dream of is unreal... until you bring it into your reality. Stay with me...

Quantum physics tells us that everything – you, me and the kitchen sink – is all made up of energy, and that everything is connected to everything else. The water in the ocean, the clouds in the sky, the plants, trees, bugs, animals and everything else comes from the same source and returns to it. Thoughts and feelings are also energy, so everything we think and feel has the potential to influence everything and everyone on the planet. In this way, we create our own reality, because mind rules over matter.

Everything that has been created by humans first existed in the imagination. Everything you see now was once an inert piece of quantum possibility floating around in the realm of human imagination until, one day, it was called forth into the realms of reality.

'Reality is merely an illusion, albeit a very persistent one.' – Albert Einstein

Everyone perceives their own life and the lives of everyone else differently. How you perceive your life determines your reality. You have the power to be, and to feel, however you choose, regardless of your background, financial status, education, gender and so on. You process around 60-70,000 thoughts per day, and most of them are the same as the thoughts you had the day before. The same thoughts result in the same choices, the same choices in the same behaviours, the same behaviours in the same experiences and round and round you go. You can stick to the path of least resistance and continue being where you are and who you are; after all, it is familiar, often comfortable, and is perfectly fine. The point I am trying to make is that you have choices, including the choice to keep doing what you are doing. There is no judgement being made here, but if you would like change to happen in your life – be it something momentous or just a little tweak or adjustment – it is perfectly possible in the quantum realm.

Chapter Fourteen

The power of suggestion

'Raise your words, not your voice. It is rain that grows flowers, not thunder.'
– Rumi

Hypnosis, whether induced by a clinical practitioner or DIY, as in self-hypnosis, is based on the power of suggestion. If you recall, the dictionary definition of hypnosis suggests that hypnosis contradicts the idea of free will, even though it does not. No one can be cajoled, convinced, forced or hypnotised to do anything against their will. Hypnotherapy is not a placebo. Studies using hypnosis for anaesthesia have shown that pain relief from hypnosis is quite different from a placebo effect, with evidence pointing to the fact that pain is a subjective experience affected by how it is perceived.

'What about stage hypnosis?' I hear you ask, referring to when people are forced to run around clucking like chickens. Well, there are a few schools of thought on the subject, and here I will share my own. Swathes of stage hypnotists will beg to differ, but we all have the right to an opinion, and mine is based on personal experience and observation. Stage hypnosis is entertainment. Unlike hypnotherapy, which is designed to achieve a positive therapeutic outcome, and as with any other stage show, the audience will consist of people of all ages and from all walks of life. Members of the audience will be selected to join the hypnotist on stage, and every participant will have their own reasons for wanting to take part. The selection process for participants will include a series of suggestibility tests; these people may just be curious about hypnosis and want to experience it first-hand, while some may be shy, reserved characters who have been presented with an opportunity to behave outrageously without taking responsibility for their actions. There could be highly compliant people who go on stage, those who are *game for a laugh* and then, of course, there may just be the occasional *plant*. Suggestions are made by the hypnotist to the participants, and the audience delights in their subsequent humiliation. It is a bit of fun; we all enjoy watching people do silly things. That said, hypnosis is a genuine psychological phenomenon, and most of us can be hypnotised, **but only** if we give permission.

The CIA and KGB are known to have experimented with hypnosis and mind control in the hope of creating the perfect spy or assassin, and while there are plenty of stories, conspiracy theories and published research into mind control, there has not been any concrete evidence to prove that it is possible, until now. Artificial intelligence is getting much better at reading minds, and the world's biggest players in AI are racing to develop their own mind-reading capabilities. Facebook recently announced plans for a device to enable people to type using their thoughts, and Microsoft, the US Defence Agency and Elon Musk are all believed to have their own mind-reading projects under way.

What about brainwashing?

'The process of pressurising someone into adopting radically different beliefs by using systematic and often forcible means.' (Source: https://www.lexico.com/en/definition/brainwash)

Brainwashing is a term usually perceived as a negative, and, dare I say, I also perceive it as such. However, there may be another way of looking at it.

In psychology, we study something called conditioning. Conditioning is a behaviour whereby a response becomes more frequent or more predictable in a given environment as a result of negative or positive reinforcement; reinforcement typically being a stimulus or reward for a desired response. Probably the most famous example of classical conditioning is Pavlov's dog. Pavlov knew that dogs salivate in the presence of food, and he used this in testing his theory that dogs can be conditioned to salivate at the sound of a bell and the sight of men in white lab coats in anticipation of food.

In a similar study, which was not only unethical but, quite frankly, deeply disturbing, 'Little Albert' was the participant. Watson and Rayner (1920) used this poor child (with the permission of his mother, believe it or not) to evoke a fear response to an object which was at first seen by Little Albert as completely non-threatening. Here is a brief synopsis of the sorry tale:

Little Albert, a nine-month-old baby, was given a white rat. The rat crawled up to him and wandered all around. Little Albert showed interest in the rat, but remained completely unafraid. The rat was taken away. Shortly afterwards, the researchers produced the rat again, but as they placed it next to Albert this time, they let off a loud, startling clang. Little Albert jumped and cried.

This was repeated multiple times until poor Little Albert began to cry at the mere appearance of the rat, with or without the loud clang. Albert's fear response extended to other furry creatures, like a dog and a monkey; animals that previously provoked only mild interest, but certainly not fear. The researchers taught Little Albert to be afraid.

The experiment was conducted as part of the psychologists' attempts to prove that infants are blank slates, and therefore infinitely malleable. If you are not faint of heart, you can see this cruel experiment repeated on a number of YouTube channels.

We arrive in this world with a clear mind and with pure thoughts. As we develop, we learn from our parents, caregivers, teachers, siblings and peers, mirroring those who we look up to. As we begin to experience life for ourselves, we pick up beliefs, fears and limitations from our environment that go on to form the person we are today. Is this brainwashing?

'Children must be taught how to think, not what to think.' – Margaret Mead, cultural anthropologist

Apart from our early 'programmers,' who and what else is responsible for our programming?

What about the way you talk *about* yourself and the way you talk *to* yourself?

The late, great Dr Wayne Dyer wrote and spoke a lot on the significance of the words 'I AM.' He pointed out that phrases such as *I am not smart, I am not talented, I am bad, I am not attractive, I am unloved* or *I am unworthy* repeated often enough, especially from childhood through to adulthood, are destined to become our defining self-beliefs.

Dr Dyer believed that if we become aware of negative self-talk and begin to correct ourselves, we can change our entire belief system. In fact, he wrote an entire book on the subject, *Change Your Thoughts Change Your Life*. The concept is that to become consciously aware of negative self-talk, and indeed the negative words, you speak aloud. 'I am not well,' becomes 'I am getting better,' or 'I am not clever,' becomes 'I am learning something new every day.' I am unable to do this or that because of the government, my family, my boss, my income, my education, my looks, my height, my skill set and so on becomes noticed, and you can begin to halt negative self-talk in its tracks by rephrasing your verbal and internal self-talk.

As Henry Ford once said, 'If you think you can or you think you can't, you're probably right.'

Cup half empty or cup half full?

Are you an optimist or a pessimist? Do you think positive thoughts or negative ones? Is your grass a healthy shade of green, or is it lush and much more vibrant on the other side of the fence?

No matter how you think and feel right now, you can choose to maintain the same mental attitude or you can choose to change it. It really is a choice. Irrespective of what cards you have been dealt, who has done what and whatever else has happened, you can choose to change. It is rarely possible to change other people in the way they behave, respond or act. It is not always possible to change the environment you live in, your neighbours, your family, your work colleagues or your boss. As a matter of fact, the only thing you CAN change is YOU.

If you are happy and life is wonderful, you have got this covered, so keep doing what you are doing! However, if you feel stuck, unhappy, unfulfilled or frustrated with life, then choose to change it. But then, you must make it happen. Change can be a challenge; change can be a bit uncomfortable. After all, you have practised doing what you do and being the way that you are for years now. It may not give you the results you are looking for, but it feels safe and familiar.

Exercise 10

Hello You!

(Tools required: 1x pen or pencil, 2x pieces of paper)

First of all, you are going to have a conversation with your inner critic. It will be easier than you think, as your inner critic is always chattering, questioning your decisions, making you doubt yourself and preventing you from acting on that flash of inspiration and, quite possibly, right at this moment, poopooing this exercise.

1. Beginning with the words 'I am,' start writing on one piece of paper all the negative beliefs you have about yourself. Use bullet points as opposed to long sentences. Write down your faults, your weaknesses and anything you do

not like about yourself. Start writing now before moving on to the next part of the exercise. No one else is listening or watching, so be as truthful as you like. Write until you are quite sure you have left nothing out, no stone left unturned; get it all out. If you need to flip the paper over, feel free to do so.

2. Now, find justification for each belief. Write each justification down, again using bullet points. For example, statement: 'I am not successful.' Justification: 'I have a low-paid / boring / dead-end job.' Statement: 'I am unlovable.' Justification: 'My relationships never last.'

3. Once you are finished, grab a fresh piece of paper and, beginning with the words 'I am,' write a counterstatement to each and every point. Do this regardless of if you believe the statement to be true or false. Just allow the words to flow. If you find this part tricky, just remember, your inner critic is hijacking you. Just write and keep writing. For example, statement: 'I am successful.' Justification: 'I can do anything I put my mind to.' Statement: 'I am lovable.' Justification: 'I have people (or even pets) in my life who love me.'

4. Now, take the first piece of paper with all the negative points, and without reading it over, tear it up, shred it or burn it. Do that now. (If you have chosen the latter, do I need to remind

you of possible fire hazards? Good, I thought not. Just covering bases.)

5. OK, now, sitting with the new set of positive self-beliefs, read them through one by one.

When you write things down, two things happen in your brain: storage and encoding

Storage is information learned that is easy to access and review at any time. Encoding is the first step to creating a new memory.

The parts of the brain involved with memory are the amygdala, the hippocampus, the cerebellum and the prefrontal cortex. Your amygdala is involved in emotion, your hippocampus in consolidating memories from the short-term to the long-term, your cerebellum interprets touch, vision, hearing, reasoning and control of movement and, finally, your prefrontal cortex is involved in cognitive behaviour, personality, expression, decision-making and social behaviour.

And so, now you are sitting with a piece of paper and a bunch of positive statements written on it, some of which you may not believe to be true... yet.

Remember that quote from Henry Ford?

It has been my personal experience that simply reading or repeating positive statements (affirmations) regularly has little impact. Most likely, this is because affirmations work on a conscious level, and this is where your inner critic resides. Your inner critic can be loud and can knock you clean off of your newly-erected perch. So, how can you believe the things you want to believe about yourself?

Cognitive reappraisal

This is more than just replacing your negative self-beliefs with positive ones; this is about re-examining a thought or a belief and challenging it, so that your brain begins to understand that those irritating negative thoughts have little or no ground to stand on. We are stepping things up here.

Just like anything new that you have learned or ever will learn in the future, it takes a little practise. When you were a baby learning to walk, you would have fallen down time and time again, but did it ever occur to you to give up? When you fell for the hundredth time, did your parents ever tell you to stop bothering? That it looks like walking isn't your thing, so you may as well give it up and stick with crawling? When you learned to ride a bike, swim or drive a car, did you practise? Of course you did. This is how we humans progress and get things done. This is our modus operandi.

When you become aware of negative thoughts, especially if they are repetitive, write them down and challenge them. Do it over and over again. Practise. By doing this, you are literally creating new neural pathways! You could consider patterns of negative or repetitive thinking like a vinyl record. Vinyl records have grooves, and in this scenario, the vinyl represents your brain and the grooves are your patterns, habits and habitual thinking. When a stylus (trigger) is placed on the vinyl, it traces a spiral pattern leading it from the record's outer edge to its inner diameter, following subtle grooves along the way. The more the record is played, the deeper the grooves become. If the record gets scratched, the stylus gets stuck and so does the music.

If you get stuck, try distraction. In this modern age, most of us have become really good at getting distracted; checking our phones, making calls, reading or writing emails on the go, internet surfing, social media updating and so on, but in this instance, you can use the art of distraction to your advantage. When negative patterns show up, get up and move around. Channel your energy into doing something completely unrelated to the thought or situation. Think about something else entirely. Your brain will soon forget the negative thought once it is focussed on a new task.

When using the words 'I am,' you are talking and thinking in the present tense. 'I will' implies a wish or an *intention* to do or to become, whereas 'I'll *try*' implies an expectation to fail.

Chapter Fifteen

Finding balance

'Choose a job you love, and you will never have to work a day in your life.'
– Unknown (often credited to Confucius)

Being out of balance means that the scale is tipped in favour of one area, leaving another area light.

Finding balance can prove challenging.

I happen to love what I do, and I consider myself very fortunate in this regard. Having said that, I have had a number of jobs over the years that I have had to literally drag myself out of bed for, from selling ladies' corsetry in a department store at 16, to typing tedious minutes of meetings for the Labour Party, which, unlike the name suggests, was no *party* to a 16-year-old party animal.

Was I working to live or living to work? Back in those days, I had one priority, and that was to earn enough money to fund my lifestyle. My lifestyle then consisted primarily of buying and wearing the latest fashion, consuming as much alcohol as was humanly possible and doing whatever else I could do to shock my mother, so I can now look back and say with confidence, I was working to live. Today, however, is a different story, a different set of circumstances and different priorities, yet regardless of what we do for a living, we all work to fund a lifestyle, do we not? Even for those who go 'off-grid,' leave the rat race, build a shack in the forest and live off the land, work still needs to be done in order to survive, or else they'll starve and fade into oblivion. It is a case of finding the right balance.

If you work at a job you loathe day in and day out just to survive, what does that say to you and what does that say about you? Yes, you are a trouper, a provider, a conscientious worker and a valuable member of the community, and perhaps even the planet, but could there be anything you could do to improve the way you *feel* about what you do? I wonder, could you become more mindful, more present in those precious moments that you work so hard for? If you are the breadwinner supporting a family, large or small, instead of bringing your work home with you (literally or figuratively), what if you were to leave your woes at the front door and become more involved in what it is you actually go to work for? You may call it spending *quality time*.

Some of you reading this may well be thinking, *It's ok for her to say that, but I have this and that to deal with. My life is more complicated, more demanding and I have no other choice. I have too much to lose...* Well, I can only come at this from my own perspective, and from that of the people I have loved and still love, been inspired by, worked with and worked for, and tell you that time flies. Life may seem as though it drags and stands still when you are doing things you would rather not be doing, but time waits for no man, woman or child. It seems like yesterday that my daughter and my son were sitting on my lap, and now my lap is full of grandchildren and I cannot quite believe where the time has gone.

My mother worked all her life as a single parent, which was virtually unheard of back in the '70s. She did what she needed to do to keep us, to feed us, to clothe us and to make us happy, but did we appreciate it at the time? To be honest, not really. How could we? We were far too young and carefree. Then, guess what happened next? Time happened. As I write these words, my mother, having enjoyed perhaps 10 years of retirement, fell victim to dementia. Her memories are fading fast, and if she were able to have a wish granted, it would probably be to recapture time. Time is all we have, so spend it wisely.

Family Life

Family life is not very often like the adverts we see on TV, reality shows or the movies, and hopefully not too much like the soap operas, either. The *real* reality for most people is that family life has ups and downs; it can be wonderful, but it can also be tough. Trials, tribulations, hard times, good times, sad times, overwhelming times, happy and joyful times. Whether you are bringing up a family or are part of a family, family life can be challenging and rewarding all in the same day.

Is it possible to find a work-life balance?

Yes, if you work smarter, not harder. Love or loathe this phrase, it speaks volumes. To me, it has nothing to do with how *smart* you are, or how much of your workload you delegate, but everything to do with making the hours that you do work count. By learning to become more self-aware, you will be more able to discover your strengths and build on them, so that you can reach your goals in the quickest and most efficient way possible, and still have *time* to live your life!

When you work smarter instead of harder, you free up more 'you time,' more family time and more time to rest and to think clearly; to do the things you enjoy. Taking life a bit slower during recreational time results in you spending more time in your moments.

It's a matter of simple equations:

1. Good night's sleep = clear mind in the morning

2. Clear mind in the morning = good choices and

decisions made during the day

3. Good choices and decisions made during the day = calm mind and more time to relax in the evening and at the weekend

4. More time to relax in the evening and at the weekend = more present to enjoy the moments you go to work for

5. More present to enjoy the moments you work for = work-life balance

'Sometimes you will never know the value of a moment until it becomes a memory.' **– Theodor Seuss Geisel, aka Dr Seuss**

Taking time out is important for your mental health and overall wellbeing. You do not have to travel afar, or travel anywhere for that matter, just step away from the hustle and bustle of everyday life for a time to connect with the people you love and the things that matter to you most. Taking time out to reconnect is a time for relaxation, a time to unwind, de-stress and to be more YOU, and when the holiday is over, you return to everyday life with more focus. You will be more productive, creative and inspired, not to mention the proud owner of a suitcase filled with happy memories.

You may feel that you are unable to take time off because things would fall apart if you were to go away, or that someone else might take your place or the credit for all the hard work you have put in. You could lose clients, miss important calls or meetings, lose money, miss an opportunity or even get fired. If this sounds like you, you need a holiday! Obviously, I am not talking about throwing in the proverbial towel and handing in your resignation, but take a break, a long weekend, a week or two weeks, and if you can unplug from technology during those times, even better. Give yourself permission to take time out. After all, the only person who can truly look after your mental, emotional and physical wellbeing is you.

In 2019, a full-time employee in the UK has the legal right to 28 days holiday each year. If you are self-employed, you will no doubt need to put money aside in order to pay yourself while you are on holiday, but either way, it is at your own peril if you decide against investing in some quality R&R. How does that saying go again? Oh yes, 'Because you're worth it.'

When I was a teenager, not many people had holidays abroad, and if it were not for the fact that I came from, and still had family in, America, I very much doubt I would have had the opportunity to travel abroad and, consequently, I would never have developed a passion for it. My son, on the other hand, is of the new generation of insatiable travellers. No sooner had he left university, he and his friends donned backpacks and were outward bound. During the year that he was travelling, I learned an awful lot about control – mostly about being stripped of it. I spent many a long day and night worrying, fretting, crying and trawling social media, or glued to the news and more or less stalking everyone who knew him. He still works and travels abroad, but now instead of worrying (much), I admire him immensely and feel excited for him every time he ventures off into a new life experience. There is not much of the world he has not seen, and what corners are left, I have no doubt he will visit. They say that there is no better education than travel, but I would say that there is no better education than experience. When you experience life in whatever way you choose, you learn, you create memories and, at the end of our days, memories are what we are left with.

Is there a role for hypnotherapy in creating a healthy work-life balance?

Of course! But then, you knew I would say that.

Exercise 11

System reboot

Giving your mind a system reboot is a wonderful way to ensure that you are functioning, both at work and at play, to your full potential, which consequently creates more time and space in your life.

You can do this exercise any time of day and anywhere you can find 10-20 minutes' peace and quiet (maybe even in your lunch break):

1. Sit or lie down and get comfortable. If you are sitting, sit upright with your feet flat on the floor and your hands flat on your thighs.

2. Close your eyes and begin to breathe very slowly and deeply, in through your nose and out through your mouth. Make the breath longer and deeper, breathing in a sense of calm and breathing out any tension or stress in your body.

3. Allow your thoughts to come and go; imagine them as clouds in the sky, passing through. Acknowledge your thoughts; don't try to push them out, but do not focus on them or give them attention. Just let them float by. Your thoughts will not stop, but will begin to slow down naturally.

4. As you quieten the mind, you may be more aware of sounds inside or outside the room. These sounds will fade into the background and help relax you even more.

5. If at any time your thoughts invade your peaceful moment, bring your attention back to your breath and count in for seven, out for 11, slow and deep. The steady rhythm will help you to centre.

Stay in this relaxed state for 10-20 minutes, and then allow yourself to come back to full waking consciousness.

Consider using this time to connect with your creativity, to find solutions to a problem. Try not to apply logic or reasoning, or to dwell on the problem itself, and just ask your mind for the solution. Keep it simple and let the answers come to you.

Chapter Sixteen

Wealth

'If you approach the ocean with a cup, you can only take away a cupful. If you approach it with a bucket, you can take away a bucketful.'
– Ramana Maharshi, sage

The word 'wealth' comes from the old English word '*Wela*,' meaning 'happiness and prosperity in abundance.'

What does wealth mean to you?

Think about it for a moment. In fact, if you have a pen and paper to hand, I invite you to write down your personal interpretation of *wealth* in as many (or as few) words as you can think of in 30 seconds. Go...

I would hazard a guess that most people will have written down (or thought of) one, some or all of the following:

1. Money

2. Personal possessions, like watches and jewellery

3. First-class world travel

4. Homes, boats and cars

5. Family

6. Health

7. Love

Of course, wealth means different things to different people. In the third world, for example, wealth is often measured in land, crops or livestock. In troubled and war-torn countries, freedom may be considered wealth, as could education, access to clean water or electricity. H.W. Charles, author of *The Money Code*, is quoted as saying, '*Wisdom* is really the key to wealth. With great wisdom, comes great wealth and success. Rather than pursuing wealth, pursue wisdom.'

Today, there is something like 280 trillion USD of wealth in circulation (I am using US Dollars, as it is the most popular currency in which to measure monetary value). This estimate does not represent physical cash, but *wealth*. Furthermore, it is said that just 1% of the population holds the majority of this wealth, and that if it were to be redistributed equally among everyone, it would take just one generation for it all to end up back in the hands of that 1%. *Interesting*. The theory here is that the poor are not poor because they lack money, but because they lack the means of making money. A sudden influx of cash is more likely to be spent quickly rather than invested prudently, therefore, the wealth could not be sustained. Similarly, the wealthy are thought to be wealthy because they know how to produce the goods and services that people want to buy, hence their advantage is not hindered by taking their wealth away. The wealthy-minded will simply find a way to become wealthy again.

'Capital goes where it is welcome and stays where it is well treated.' – **Walter Bigelow Wriston, commercial banker**

Is it unrealistic to expect people to live in financial harmony? Perhaps.

If everyone on the planet had one billion dollars, the dollar would be worthless. If everyone had just one dollar, the dollar would be useless.

What about the ideology of communism? Communism is supposed to be an economic and political system whereby everyone is equal, the ultimate goal of which is to create a classless society. However, you have only to look at China today, which has more billionaires in government than any other country in the world, referred to as the 'Red Aristocracy,' to see how communism is working out for the average Chinese citizen.

Money itself is just paper or metal. In fact, most of the money today is even less than that; it is digital, existing solely on computers and hard drives. And what the heck is crypto currency and Bitcoin anyway? If you go to buy a house, you do not physically go to the bank and withdraw a few hundred thousand pounds in cold, hard cash and hand it to over to the person selling the house (at least not under normal circumstances), you have it transferred digitally. You cannot see it, so where is it? You shop online, you push a button and the money magically disappears from your bank account and arrives with the merchant in the blink of an eye. It boggles my mind.

Before money was invented, people bartered, e.g. 'My goat for your two chickens,' that kind of thing. So, in essence, not much has changed. We still operate by means of exchange.

This begs the question, if money itself is no longer really *real*, why are so many of us still fixated on having it?

According to the Law of Attraction, money is energy. I am well aware that there are plenty of people who really do enjoy the tangible variety; the look of cash, the feel of it, the sound of it and even the smell of it. There are those who like to splash it around, have rolls of it in their pockets or keep it locked away in banks, safes and vaults, but ultimately, it is what money *buys* that makes most of us tick. It comes down to lifestyle.

Trivia question: would you rather be rich in a poor country or poor in a rich country?

What do you believe about money? By this, I mean do you believe money is good or evil? Do you believe anyone can be wealthy or that privilege is reserved for the lucky few? Do you have to work hard for money, or can it come easily?

When you examine your own beliefs about money and wealth, you will gain insight into why you are where you are financially. If you spend a lot of time worrying about not having enough money or running out of money, your core belief is that money is scarce. If, on the other hand, you are comfortable and always seem to have enough money, your core belief is that you will always have either enough or more than enough. If you struggle with finances, if money seems to run through your hands like water, if you live payday to payday or hand to mouth, your core beliefs surrounding money could be what is holding you back or blocking you from moving towards financial freedom. Keep saying 'I can't,' and your subconscious mind will accept it. Try saying, 'I can,' or ask, 'How can I?' as this will keep your subconscious mind on the ball, weighing up possibilities and looking out for opportunities.

Exercise 12

The audit

(Tools required: 1x Pen / Pencil, 1x paper)

1. In one word, summarise your current financial situation.

2. In one sentence, write down the reason for your answer.

3. In one paragraph, summarise why you <u>believe</u> you are in your current situation.

Examine your beliefs. Be completely open and honest with yourself. Now, you may have some wonderful words and sentences on your piece of paper, you may have a few negative ones, or you might have chosen not to play along and write anything down at all. It is your prerogative. However, if you have answered all of the questions, you will have a snapshot of how you truly feel about money and wealth. Is there anything you can improve upon? Is it possible for you to have a better relationship with money? If so, how? Brainstorm it. Throw some ideas around, meditate on it, sleep on it, blow off some cobwebs and order your subconscious mind to get working on ideas and inspiration. Even if you are financially set for life, it pays well to wonder.

Abundance – now we're talking

To be abundant is to have a lot of something, the opposite of which is *lack*.

The Law of Attraction states that what you think about most becomes your reality; you literally attract that which you focus on. This being the case, if you are constantly thinking that you can never make ends meet, are stuck in a dead-end job, that people are untrustworthy or unkind, that you have a condition that prevents you from doing what you really want to do and so on, you will look for evidence to support your belief.

You are always broke, you buy a lottery ticket, you listen as the winning numbers are announced, you know you never win – someone else always wins – and your numbers are not called out. You see? You were right. You stop buying lottery tickets.

To have an abundant mentality is to know there is abundance of everything and enough for everyone, so someone else's gain is never your loss. You know that you can just go get your own piece of the proverbial pie.

'Where your attention goes, energy flows.'

Have you ever noticed that when you're away on holiday or relaxing in the garden on a warm summer's day, you stop focussing on aches and pains or stresses and strains that might have been plaguing you earlier? Then, no sooner do you land back home, or Monday morning arrives, than it all floods back again. It is hardly surprising, because when you are in a state of relaxation, you are giving your immune system a rest also. Of course, this is not always the case, as some people take stress with them everywhere that they go.

Take a holiday scenario. You may know someone like this, or perhaps you are the one who gets anxious on or preparing for holiday, worrying about what could go wrong, what you may forget to pack, how busy the motorway will be, if you'll miss your flight, if the weather will be too hot or too cold, if you'll have enough money, if you'll be bitten half to death by mosquitoes or contract salmonella or worse. This is called catastrophising, and most of us will have catastrophised at one time or another, predicting or seeing a situation considerably worse than it actually is or could be, and, more often than not, everything turns out to perfectly fine with no catastrophe ever having occurred.

So, here we have two very different people going on the exact same holiday:

Holiday maker #1 – red-faced, high blood pressure, sweating profusely, dropping tickets and tripping over their own excess baggage; running late, last one in the slowest queue, moaning to fellow travellers or anyone else within earshot, allocated a seat next to a screaming child on the plane.

Holiday maker #2 – relaxed and calm, smiling at fellow travellers, single light suitcase on wheels; extra check-in desk opens upon arrival, first in the queue, unexpected upgrade, headphones on, kick back, happy days.

You are a walking, talking, living, breathing ball of energy, and so is everything and everyone around you. We all emitted from the same original spark that created our universe. Whatever your theory of creation may be, everything had to start somewhere and begin with something, and so, whatever happened, happened, and billions of years later, here you are, thinking and feeling separate to everything and everyone else. Surely, all life is connected to all other life, because we all exist in the same space in time.

The burning question, then: can you literally think things into existence?

Everything that exists in the material world was first a thought, a vision, an idea or a flash of inspiration. The trick, then, must be how to do it. First of all, your thoughts need to be strong enough to convert things into reality, and by strong enough, I mean you must believe that you can achieve them.

Chapter Seventeen

Success

'I am the greatest, I said that even before I was.'
– Muhammad Ali

When I was at senior school, the boys took metalwork and woodwork classes and girls attended needlework and home economics. In sixth form, the girls were offered a bonus subject, touch typing. I tried my best to sew, but everything I made fell apart. I followed recipes to the letter, yet still my cakes sunk and my shepherd's pies burned. I left school sure of one thing, though: I could type.

I longed to build a wooden stool with a rattan, woven seat, like the boys did. I could just imagine the beaming faces of proud parents presented with these beautiful handmade pieces of furniture. The stools these lads produced looked solid enough to last a lifetime; good enough to be handed down to the next generation of future craftsmen. I suspect that these bespoke pieces took pride of place in sitting rooms across the country, with mother and father showing them off smugly to all who visited. My humble offering to rewire a plug from a household appliance, or a slice of a lopsided Victoria sponge served from a recycled biscuit tin, was less of an heirloom. Determined not to end up spending my adult life browsing through sewing patterns at C&H fabrics, I left school and moved to London.

Despite the sex discrimination prevalent in the '70s, I achieved excellent exam results, including an A for my rendition of a dissected red pepper, which shocked the Art teacher as much as it shocked me. My idea of success back then was going on to land a half-decent job, which, happily, I did.

I have had many successes since then, as well as one or two dismal failures, I must be honest, but as a self-proclaimed optimist, I have perfected the art of selective memory, and so I file all botches and disasters to the rear of my memory storeroom under 'miscellaneous.' I jest, of course, as making mistakes is part of what it takes to become successful. If you never made a mistake, it would be impossible to learn or to improve. Moreover, if you failed to learn from your mistakes, you would continue to make them over and over again. Making mistakes helps build confidence and resolve; you develop wisdom and good judgement, which you can then teach and share with others.

Predictability

Imagine if you knew exactly how every moment of every day would unfold; if there were no unknowns, and everything was absolutely certain. Whether you were rich and successful or poor and unfortunate, every day would unfold exactly as the last. No change, no improvement, no surprises and nothing to look forward to; Groundhog Day. I wonder if anyone would even bother to get out of bed.

Success comes in many guises; in business, academia, fame and fortune. Success is raising a family, being able to produce a family, helping to save the planet, building something, creating or inventing something, breaking a bad habit, climbing a mountain, sailing across the Atlantic Ocean or overcoming an illness. Success is achieving the things that you desire.

Exercise 13

A little ego never hurt anyone

I invite you to take a few moments to reflect on your successes so far, large or small. Be kind to yourself, let your ego do the talking. You may want to start writing a list; write everything down as a reminder of how amazing you are. You began with a breath, and here you are today. Congratulations on making it this far. Now, how far can you go? Irrespective of where you think you are or where you think you should be headed, know that you are headed somewhere, and wherever that somewhere is, make sure it the best it can be, because only you can do that.

Now that you are aware of your successes to date, hopefully you are pondering the future. You will agree that in order to be successful, you must have a clear vision of what it is that you wish to be successful at. It doesn't have to be one thing, it can be lots of things. However, focussing on one area at a time and working through your list tends to work well.

'What this game needs is a goal!'

Life goals are most likely to relate to one or all of the following areas:

- Health and Wellness

- Personal development

- Relationships / Love / Friendships

- Creating more free time

- Finances / Wealth

- Career / Business

Perhaps you have more goals or other goals that you would like to aim for; the important thing here is to name them. Write them down, look at them regularly, adjust them if necessary and give yourself a date to achieve them. This is vital, as a human tendency is to procrastinate, and procrastination fuels feelings of self-doubt and undermines self-confidence, so go forth with confidence, even if you have to fake it at first.

OK, so now that you know what you are aiming for, it would be prudent to take a good look at where you are right now in relation to where you want to be.

My children used to love the *Where's Wally?* books by Martin Handford. Wally, or Waldo, as he is known in the US, who is distinguishable by his red-and-white-striped shirt, bobble hat and round glasses, is cunningly hidden within a plethora of intricately detailed scenes. The challenge is to spot Wally as quickly as possible, and sometimes you spot him quickly, while other times he completely evades you. The illustrations in these wonderful, mind-boggling books create an optical illusion, based on the brain trying to interpret what we see and make sense of it according to our reality. When you do finally manage to find Wally, your brain rewards you with a surge of dopamine. Success, no matter how big or small, feels good.

Exercise 14

Reinventing the wheel

(Tools required: 1x pen / pencil, 1x steel jaw)

Where are you right now in relation to where you want to be? You may be closer than you thought, or a million miles away and you need to see it, no frills.

A tried and tested way to see where you are in various areas of your life is by using the 'Wheel of Life,' which is an oldie but a goodie. The concept was originally created way back in the 1960s by Paul J. Meyer, founder of the Success Motivation® Institute, and although well-known and often used, it remains the gold standard and well worth revisiting every so often.

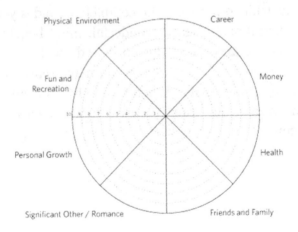

On a scale of 1-10, with 1 being unhappy and 10 being very happy, you draw a solid line that corresponds to where you are at this moment (e.g. if you are working so much that you have no time for fun and recreation, you may draw a solid line at no.1).

Gradually work your way around the areas of your life, drawing lines that represent your reality.

The finished article may end up looking something like this:

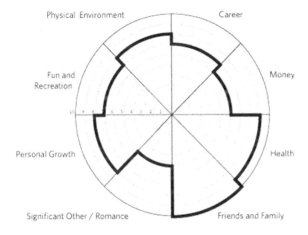

Not only does this exercise give you a visual representation of where you are in these areas of your life, but it also begs the question, if your wheel were to take off now, how would it roll?

It is a matter of balance, and balance is everything.

Another way to demonstrate your current position would be to use a standard bar chart method.

Being aware of the areas in your life that need work, and then working on them accordingly, will pave a smoother road along your journey to success.

A couple of tips before you take off along that road:

1. Eradicate blame. Blaming anyone else for where you are or who you are, regardless of the role they might have played, is futile and an enormous waste of your valuable energy.

2. Eradicate resentment. Holding onto feelings of resentment means you are stuck in the past, and living in the past serves only to hold you back from moving forward.

Bon voyage!

Chapter Eighteen

Magnetism

*'Everything is energy and that's all there is to it.
Match the frequency of the reality you want and you
cannot help but get that reality. It can be no other
way. This is not philosophy. This is physics.'*
– Albert Einstein

Magnetism, the Law of Attraction, manifestation... call it what you will. I often go between all three, as you might have noticed throughout this book, yet the fundamentals are the same, which is to intentionally create and bring into your reality the things you desire. Regardless of your point of view being spiritual or scientific, we can all agree that there are several universal laws. The Law of Gravity, the Law of Cause and Effect, the Law of Polarity, electromagnetism, the Law of Vibration, the Law of Relativity and so on.

The Law of Attraction has had a lot of publicity in recent years, especially since the release of the movie and publication of the book, *The Secret*. Authors such as Dr Wayne Dyer, Bob Proctor, Deepak Chopra and Eckhart Tolle, and celebrities like Oprah Winfrey, Will

Smith and Jim Carey have all contributed to the theory being brought into the mainstream. Back in the early 1900s, we had mavericks such as Napoleon Hill, Dale Carnegie and Earl Nightingale, but the concept of the Law of Attraction has been around for even longer. Incantations, chanting, mantras and prayer are all ancient forms of manifestation.

'Call those things which are not as though they were.' (Romans 4:17)

Regardless of your religious persuasion, it may be worth considering whether or not these words hold any weight when it comes to the art of manifestation. A spiritual explanation for the Law of Attraction and manifestation is that by aligning yourself to source energy or the universe, you can manifest your desires into physical reality. The premise is that we are all made up of energy, and this energy is the same energy that was emitted from the original spark or big bang. Energy is a frequency, and as frequencies can change, we surely must be capable of changing our frequency with positive thoughts, gratitude, feelings, motivation or beliefs.

As with the Law of Magnetism, energy attracts. What we attract depends on where and how we focus our attention, so if you focus on what you do not have or do not want, the Law of Attraction will deliver more of that. Bear in mind, your subconscious mind does not distinguish between a negative or a positive thought, nor does it judge your thoughts or decisions, and more importantly, your subconscious mind does not differentiate between a real event or an imagined one. The language of the subconscious mind is emotion. When your thoughts are accompanied by an emotion, a feeling or a strong enough belief, they can manifest into your reality.

I happen to like science. I like hard facts, research studies and *proof* of things, yet I am and have always been open-minded. I have been called opinionated (by my husband and children, mostly), and so I try hard not to dismiss new information and ideas out of hand. And when I look back at the things I have and what I have accomplished so far in my life, there is a common thread: me. I made it happen. All of it. The things that were going on around me might have seemed random and sometimes unjust or unfair, but it was what I did with those *things* and how I responded to those events that have created my reality. I am a manifestor, as are you.

A more mainstream explanation for manifestation – for bringing things into reality – is that when you are focussed on what you want and believe that it is possible, you are more likely to take risks, to step out of your comfort zone and follow your dream. People who have a strong self-belief are more open to opportunities and possibilities. On the other hand, when you do not believe that something is possible, you are more likely to let opportunities pass you by. If you believe you are undeserving or incapable, you are sabotaging your chances of happiness and fulfilment. By becoming more aware of your self-talk and more in touch with your feelings, you can reverse negative patterns and create better ones. One good thing leads to another, and the direction of a life can go from a downward spiral to an upward ascent. Research on optimism shows that optimists enjoy better health, greater happiness and more success in their lives. Optimists tend to focus their thoughts on success and will minimise their failures. A fundamental foundation of modern-day therapy is about shifting your limiting beliefs and negative self-talk, so that you can change your life and move forward in a more positive way.

So, how can you move from self-doubt to self-belief, and bring the things that you really want into your life?

First of all, you need to be clear on what it is you really want. Not to be confused with what you *need*, because if you are in *need*, it implies that you are in a state of lack, and so are likely to attract more of the same. Be specific. Rather than saying that you want money, because let's face it, you could focus on wanting money, find a shiny new penny on the floor and Hey Presto, you got what you wanted. You could say that you want to meet your perfect partner, but what qualities or features would you like them to possess? If you want a better house, car or a wider circle of friends, get specific. Create a beautiful picture of what it is you really want. When you have a clear picture in your mind, start believing it. Without belief, what you have is an unfulfilled dream, a wish. You may as well whistle in the wind.

The Bigger Picture

You may be familiar with the concept of vision boards. Interior designers use these all the time, otherwise referred to as mood boards, to lay out their vision of the room or space they intend to create. They will choose colour swatches, paints, materials and fabrics, cut out pictures from magazines of furniture, rugs, flowers and ornaments to gain inspiration, and then set out their plan; their vision. Once they have the vision laid out, they go on to create it. There is no doubt in the designer's mind that the room will be created, and very often it will turn out just as they had visualised or better. There is no reason for them to doubt the end result. If funding were an issue or if materials were unavailable, a designer would simply improvise until they have created their vision and it had become manifest. They have total belief in themselves to get the job done to their precise specification.

Many successful entrepreneurs and business-people speak of starting their businesses and creating multi-million-dollar companies from nothing because they had a vision, followed it and saw it through to the end. They steadfastly and resolutely pushed forward with their plans, keeping their eye and mental focus on the big picture. Celebrities like Oprah Winfrey, Jim Carey, Katy Perry and Will Smith are all said to have used vision boards to bring their goals and visions into reality. Over the years, I have had the privilege of working with professional and semi-professional sportsmen and sportswomen using hypnotherapy to supercharge their success. For competitive sportspeople, it is imperative that they visualise winning. If they were to visualise themselves losing, their performance would suffer accordingly. It does not take much imagination to predict the outcome of a game if the team have been subjected to a barrage of negativity from their coach. Your coach is your internal dialogue. You are constantly giving yourself a team talk, so are you going out there to win or to lose?

In psychology, this is called *mental rehearsal.* Mental rehearsal is using your imagination to visualise every aspect of performing a task without physically doing it. It has been shown that visualisation sends the same signals from the brain to the muscles as those that are used when performing the physical task. Athletes like Muhammad Ali, Tiger Woods, Jessica Ennis-Hill, Wayne Rooney and Jonny Wilkinson are all said to use visualisation in order to be at the top of their game. Rugby legend Jonny Wilkinson said, 'You are creating the sights and sounds and smells, the atmosphere, the sensation, and the nerves, right down to the early morning wake-up call and that feeling in your stomach. It helps your body to get used to performing under pressure.'

A Stanford University study back in 1993 showed that using visualisation under hypnosis enabled gymnasts to execute complex moves that they had been working on all year. With the aid of hypnosis, the gymnasts eliminated timing errors, increased their flexibility and improved their overall strength. Hypnosis is used regularly in professional sport, in cricket, soccer, archery, athletics, basketball and weightlifting. In fact, you would probably be hard pushed to find any sportsperson or successful businessperson who does not use creative visualisation in order to be at the top of their game. So, if you have a vision of how you would like to your life to be, and a strong belief that you can achieve it, would it not be a good idea to bring it into physical form with some empowering imagery? There is no need to lay out a vision of your entire future, although of course you can if you want to, but display images, inspirational quotes and anything else that represents the things you desire. The future can be next week, next month, a year or ten years from now. You should update your vision board when things on it have been achieved, goals met and dreams manifested. Keep it up-to-date, uplifting and exciting. The most important thing is that you must believe you can achieve the images you display. Simply sticking up pictures of things you have little faith will materialise is unlikely to produce results.

Now, no article on the subject of manifesting would be complete without considering the power of gratitude.

Mind your manners

Most of us are taught from a very young age how and when to show gratitude; continually being reminded to say 'thank you' until it becomes deeply embedded, programmed. I remember one Christmas, my grandmother gave my sister a yellow cape with Broderie Anglaise trim and matching shower cap as a gift. There was no need for words, as my sister's face said everything. I, of course, laughed like a hyena, but with one cutting glance from our mother, our programmed response was triggered. We bit our lips. 'Thank you,' my sister mumbled. 'Say it like you mean it please,' my red-faced mother scowled. She mumbled again, but of course she could not mean it, because she did not *feel* it. Gratitude means to *feel* grateful. Feigning gratitude will not cut ice.

(NB: the following Christmas, I received a book from said grandmother, *How to Sew Your Own Patchwork Quilt*, at which my sister fell over laughing. Karma joined us for Christmas that year.)

Gratitude is a big deal, and today, it is big business. Where once you would have found a modest selection of floral 'thank you' cards, you can now find everything from books and journals to pencil cases and water bottles emblazoned with gratitude-inspired mottos and quotations.

Psychologists explain gratitude as, 'A cognitive-affective state that is typically associated with the perception that one has received a personal benefit that was not intentionally sought after, deserved, or earned but rather because of the good intentions of another person.' (Emmons & McCullough, 2003.) A bit wordy, but legible. A more liberated view from a New Age theorist could be, 'Gratitude is the doorway to abundance.'

Is being grateful the same as being thankful?

In a nutshell, gratitude is a *feeling* and being thankful is an *act* (thanks for nothing, Grandma).

Have you ever felt hard done by or down in the dumps, and some (un)helpful soul quips, 'Never mind, just look at all the things you do have to be grateful for!'

Although the phrase is usually delivered with good intent, in that moment it can be plain irritating. Being reminded that you have another foot when you've just broken one is unlikely to boost one's mood.

I am reminded of Monty Python's *Life of Brian* and the song, Always Look on the Bright Side of Life, yet there is some solid evidence out there that supports a positive association between gratitude, thankfulness and wellbeing.

A study of couples found that when they took the time to express gratitude towards their partner, both parties felt more positive towards each other and in their relationship overall. Employers who show gratitude to their workforce report greater performance in productivity and employee satisfaction. Customers and consumers who are shown gratitude, and indeed who are *rewarded* for their valued custom, are more likely to provide positive reviews, refer friends and family and return to purchase again in the future.

In being able to manifest the things you desire, it would be prudent to apply some gratitude. A study by the National Institutes of Health in Maryland, USA, found that when you feel gratitude, your hypothalamus produces an extra dose of dopamine. Dopamine, your brains happy chemical, gives you a natural high. When we experience a rush of dopamine, we want more of it, and so become motivated to do more of what made us feel good! Ipso facto.

‘When you are grateful, fear disappears and abundance appears.’ – Tony Robbins.

Exercise 15

Magnetise

1. Make yourself comfortable, close your eyes and begin that wonderful deep diaphragmatic breathing. As you breathe in, count slowly to seven. Breathe in deeply, expanding your abdomen as you fill your lungs to full capacity. When you breathe out, breathe out to the count of 11, always making sure that your OUT breath is longer than your IN breath. Keep going with this breath, counting in for seven and out for 11. Being aware of where your thoughts are drifting and when they drift, come back to your breath and count. Seven in, 11 out.

2. When you become aware of a 'slowing down,' begin to think of something or someone you feel grateful for, past, present or future. Keep thinking until you land on a thought so wonderful, you begin to feel it in your body. Notice where you feel it. Expand it, make the feeling bigger and brighter, see what you see and hear what you hear; use all your senses to embrace the *feeling*. Allow the feeling to swell. Soak it up. If you are not smiling already, SMILE. Open your eyes. Nothing like a good dopamine rush.

Manifesting is about YOU; it is not about anyone else. The only control you have is over yourself. Your choices, your decisions; the way you respond, react, behave or communicate. Manifesting is not about manipulating other people or other people's lives, and it is not even about your environment, as trying to manipulate or control those things would be as futile as trying to control the weather. Manifesting is not wishful thinking. It would be a fruitless task to sit on your backside and wish for a big lottery win without buying a ticket, or to visualise living in a mansion or to appear on stage without taking the necessary action to get there.

Lights, camera, ACTION!

<u>Lights</u> = flash of inspiration, aka 'lightbulb moment'

<u>Camera</u> = the vision or image

<u>Action</u> = do something about it!

In order for something to take a quantum leap from idea to reality, some sort of action is required.

Inspiration. This wonderful word can be traced back to the Latin *'Inspirare'* ('to breathe or blow into') and *'Spiritu'* ('in spirit'). The wonderful author, Michael Bond, said that the inspiration for Paddington Bear came to him while he was in London's Selfridges shopping, and he saw a single bear on a shelf in the toy department: 'Coming across a small bear when I took shelter in Selfridges one snowy Christmas Eve was just such a million-to-one chance. Had there been two bears, I might have given them a passing glance, but I could hardly ignore one bear all by itself.'

JK Rowling came up with the inspiration for Harry Potter when she was on a crowded train from Manchester to London. Everything that has been created by man, woman or child began as an idea. The wheel, the compass, the steam engine, the lightbulb, the telephone, computers, space travel, air travel, navigating the globe, you name it; it all started as an inspired idea.

You may have noticed that I included the word 'child' in the above statement. Children are incredibly creative and inventive, perhaps due to the fact that they have not yet been bound by limitations, so they have the benefit of not knowing what is not possible. Children grow up listening to stories and fairy tales about magic and the wonder of life, they see technology doing all sorts of amazing things, and so as far as they are concerned, any problem can be solved. And if they are told that it cannot be done, they simply ask: '*Why?*'

'He who asks a question is a fool for five minutes, he who does not ask a question remains a fool forever.' – Chinese Proverb

Can you manifest for other people?

No, it is impossible to manifest YOUR desires for other people. The clue is in the sentence. Even though you might feel absolutely certain what someone else wants or needs, you are not them and their vision will be entirely different to yours, every time, without exception.

Can you manifest bad things?

Well, yes, for yourself you can, but why would you?

Can you manifest bad things for other people?

No, but also yes, the caveat being that the person you wish bad things upon must want those things for themselves. So, if said person is not aligned with what you are trying to attract for them, it is a non-starter, not to mention a terrific waste of your precious energy. I just had an interesting, if not somewhat morbid, thought. Imagine if bad people could wish bad things on other bad people, and bring those bad things into reality with nothing more than a thought. Would it end all wars? Intriguing, but let's move on.

What is standing in the way of you getting the things you want in life?

Could it be you? You may be thinking, *I know exactly what I want, but it's still not happening for me!* You have done the meditating, the mindfulness, recited daily affirmations, created a glorious vision board, reminded yourself how grateful you are for the things you already have and still, nothing. No change. No dreams fulfilled. Nada. Revisit your core beliefs. Look at yourself square in the face, and ask yourself what needs to change. Meditate on it, sleep on it, think about it and be honest with yourself. Answers will follow. You may not always like the answers, but they will come. Every time.

Know your limits

For me, this saying has got to be one of the most negative self-fulfilling prophecies of all time. The only occasion I can think of when it is a positive statement, is when it comes to drinking and driving. It also reminds me of a hilarious sketch from BBC's *Harry Enfield Show* back in the '90s, *Women, Know Your Limits!* I realise that there are limits in life. For instance, I am limited in my ability to go 12 rounds in the ring with Mike Tyson, or man a rocket to the International Space Station to carry out urgent repairs. However, extreme examples notwithstanding, there are a million and one things I could train for, study for, practise, have a good go at and ultimately achieve.

'The only limits in our life are those we impose on ourselves.' – **Bob Proctor**

Self-limiting beliefs, aka self-sabotage

Take a look at your belief system. What do you believe about success, social status, the state of the economy, the planet, love, friendship and happiness? What do you believe about yourself and what do you think you deserve out of this life?

Some, if not most, people define themselves by what they can or cannot do. Beliefs like, 'I tried that before and it didn't work out,' or 'I'm too old,' or 'I don't have the experience,' or 'I'm not that type of person,' or 'I'm too set in my ways,' or 'It's OK for *them*, they had this or that privilege or advantage...'

So, what sets you apart from anyone else? Why would *they* have more potential than you? You are your own best friend, but at times, you can be your own worst enemy and your own biggest critic, and the one who holds you back the most may well be YOU.

There are plenty of misogynistic, egotistical, narcissists out there; people who appear to possess a self-confidence that goes above and beyond reason. I can think of a world leader or two that fit that description, but then many of these individuals will actually suffer from deep-rooted inferiority complexes masked by over-inflated egos. Many celebrities, from

A-list to Z-list, are peppered with anxieties and self-esteem issues, yet people seem to hold them up as icons or success stories, until scandal hits, of course, or something worse befalls them.

In the bigger scheme of things, what matters most to you? A million in the bank? A pair of DD breast implants? A car so fast, you would need a racetrack to really appreciate it? Millions of adoring fans? Thousands of social media followers? If things like this are what drives you, that is perfectly fine! We are unique beings with individual needs, and as such are entitled to want whatever we it is we want in life and to feel great about it.

The statement, 'All men are created equal' is part of the US Declaration of Independence. Today, it would rightly read, 'All people are created equal.' This statement, however well-meant at the time, is clearly flawed, and not just today, but throughout history. Why is that?

The truth is that every person has their own unique set of strengths, as well as their own unique set of challenges that can either drive or inhibit them in achieving their life goals. A child born with a disability or into a poor, abusive or criminal home will clearly not have the same start in life as a child born healthy to a loving middle-class family, who lives in a nice home in a peaceful town. These are just facts.

In an ideal world, we would share our strengths and resolve the challenges we face together, lending helping hands to those less fortunate and being generally more altruistic and less narcissistic, all of which would go a long way towards making the world a better place for everyone. But sadly, we do not live in an ideal world. Life can be full of hard knocks, wrongdoings, injustices, abominations and discrimination, so what can you do to remove your own self-limiting beliefs and make room to become all you were destined to be – all that is possible for you to be – in spite of your circumstances?

Chapter Nineteen

Confidence and self-esteem

To have confidence is to have belief in your abilities, skills and knowledge. Self-confidence is not about feeling superior, but more an inner knowing that you are capable.

Self-esteem refers to the way you feel about yourself; the way you look, behave and think. It is a matter of how we perceive ourselves, and the perception we have of ourselves can often be based on a set of false beliefs. These beliefs may have formed in recent years or taken root in childhood. What we believe about ourselves develops; these beliefs are crafted, learned and practised, which thankfully means we can unlearn them, too.

Low self-esteem can have a huge impact on your happiness. It makes it difficult for you to recognise your strengths and the things you are actually good at. When you are busy focussing on the things you are *not* good at, this is where your energy and your attention goes, and like an uninvited party guest, it overstays its welcome. Low self-esteem depletes confidence; you could avoid trying new things, chasing your dreams, speaking up for yourself or expressing your ideas, and subsequently find yourself feeling stuck in a most uncomfortable comfort zone.

Self-confidence and self-esteem should not be confused with arrogance, nor should arrogance be confused with ego. Arrogance is to feel or to display an air of superiority, and it is most unpleasant. A paradox is that arrogant people often suffer with low self-esteem. Go figure.

What about ego? Well, ego has a bad reputation. 'He's on an ego trip,' or 'She has an enormous ego,' are commonly heard phrases, but like all things, moderation rather than size is what matters. To have an ego is also to have a sense of self. The word ego in Latin is '*I*,' meaning 'me, myself,' and let's face it, your sense of self is the identity you carry around with you all day every day, so it is important.

Ego was defined by Sigmund Freud as being a part of a trio of personality traits. He labelled them *Id*, *Super Ego* and *Ego*. The Id is the instinctive part of your mind, containing sexual and aggressive drives and hidden memories; the Super Ego operates as your moral compass, and your Ego is the more realistic part that mediates between the desires of the Id and the Super Ego. Confused? Many of his theories were and still are confusing.

In general, a confident person will possess some or all of the following qualities:

- **Composure**. Control over their emotions

- **Self-belief.** Able stand up for what they believe in, whether popular or not

- **Self-worth.** A confident person will not be easily offended

- **Decisive**. Able to make decisions and stick to them

- **Risk**. Willing to take more of a risk or step outside the box

- **Accept Mistakes**. Admit mistakes and learn from them

- **Praise**. Happy to praise others and has no need to hog the spotlight

- **Compliments**. Will happily give and accept compliments

- **Optimism**. A tendency to look at the positive rather than the negative

Someone with high self-esteem will be:

- **Balanced**. Having a balanced view of themselves, recognising their good qualities as well as their flaws

- **Aware**. Having a clear perception of self and a good understanding of others

- **Honest**. Able to form honest and healthy relationships, and less likely to stay in unhealthy ones

- **Realistic**. Less likely to be overcritical of themselves and others

- **Resilient**. Better able to handle stress and setbacks, and less likely to take things personally

- **Steadfast**. Will not accept abuse or maltreatment from others

- **Confident**. Which goes without saying

Now, the beliefs you hold about yourself may feel so deeply ingrained that you can hardly imagine being able to change them, but the good news is that they can be changed, it just takes a little work. There are several ways you can help raise your self-esteem, including hypnotherapy, but first, here are my top tips to raise self-esteem, strengthen the ego and build self-confidence:

1. Set yourself small challenges. When you have a positive experience, make a note of it. Put it somewhere you will see it often and move on to the next personal challenge.

2. Show yourself some love! Be kind to yourself. Do not blame or beat yourself up over things that might not have gone well in the past. Live more in the present and learn from the past.

3. Hold onto the positives. Your subconscious is always trying to protect you from danger, and as such it tends to remember negative experiences more than positive ones. This is called negativity bias, so always celebrate the wins!

4. Practise gratitude. Find something every day for which to be grateful, anything at all, big or small. Make this a daily habit and don't forget to *feel* it!

5. Get comfortable with the word 'no.' Low self-esteem can turn you into a 'people pleaser,' saying 'Yes,' when you really want to say 'No.' Becoming more comfortable with the word 'no' and setting healthy boundaries is key in developing self-esteem.

Your confidence might have taken a few knocks, and these knocks might have resulted in your levels diminishing over time. It could be poor academic performance, failing exams or your driving test, humiliating situations, a stressful life event, a relationship breakdown, financial problems, emotional or physical abuse, or perhaps you have lacked confidence as far back as you can remember.

Although some may argue that confidence is (in part at least) genetic, it is not my personal opinion or my experience. I believe that if you are brought up in an environment where your talents are recognised, your achievements acknowledged, you are reassured when you feel doubtful and encouraged and supported in your endeavours, you are very likely to grow up confident and with a healthy sense of self. On the contrary, if you have experienced the opposite, it is likely that you will have a low quantity of both.

Thankfully, there are lots of things you can do and plenty of techniques you can learn in order to become more confident.

Think of your mind as a garden. When you were born, your mind had the most perfect soil in which to sew the healthiest of seeds. Once sown, those seeds waited patiently to germinate until their needs were met, e.g. water, nutrients, the right temperature and a healthy environment. With learning and life experience, the seeds sown in your marvellous mind germinated and began to take root. Over time, your garden has flourished, and today, it very likely resembles something along the lines of the Botanical Gardens at Kew, or the amazing Gardens by the Bay in Singapore. Still, even in those places, you will find prickly thorns, poisonous plants and dangerous fungi, and you may even find the odd weed, which no doubt will be pulled up and destroyed before members of the public could ever notice.

When did you last pull up the weeds that have taken root in the garden of your mind? Do you tend to your garden regularly, or do you allow weeds and toxic plants to spread and take over?

Here comes the hypno bit...

Exercise 16

The Gardener

1. Find a quiet place to relax and close your eyes.

2. Notice your breathing and start to take control of it. Breathe slower and deeper. Breathe into your abdomen, in through your nose and out through your mouth.

3. On each out breath, say the words (audibly or internally), 'Deeper relaxed.'

4. Notice any areas in your body that may be holding onto tension. Breathe the tension out, 'Deeper relaxed.'

5. Let your thoughts wander until you find them taking you into a beautiful garden, any garden, but perhaps one that is familiar to you; one you

have seen or visited, or even an imaginary garden. Trust whatever comes into your mind.

6. Notice the array of colours; notice the plants, flowers, shrubs and trees. Are there any birds, butterflies or bees pollenating the flowers? Maybe in your garden there are gnomes or even fairies! Let your imagination go as wild as nature's own garden.

7. Breathe in the fragrant air. Feel the warm sun on your skin.

8. Begin walking down a path that leads to a wooden door. Notice what the path is made of; notice all the weeds that have sprung up through the cracks and crevices. All of these weeds need to be plucked out of the ground. Weeds have tiny little roots, so when you pull them up, they slide out of the soil with ease. It feels so satisfying. Keep pulling up weeds as you walk along the path. These weeds represent all the negative self-beliefs you have ever had about yourself.

9. When you reach the door, push it open and walk inside. Inside is a walled garden. Inside here, the grass is perfectly manicured, and all that stands on the grass are strong, tall trees. The trees have lush green canopies and large, solid trunks. You have an inner knowing that these strong trees have been in this place for as

long as you have been alive. These magnificent trees represent the confidence you were born with. You and everyone else that has ever lived or will ever live is born confident and self-assured. This is your birth right, the way you came into this world and your natural state of being; you feel, and you know, that anything positive you put your mind to is possible! Free from inhibition, doubt or fear.

10. Become the tree. Yes, you heard me correctly. Become that towering, strong, healthy, vibrant, living tree. Feel the strength surge through every atom of your being.

11. Stay here in this powerful space for as long as you choose, and when you feel ready, bring yourself back to full alertness.

12. Attend to your garden regularly, and prepare to grow and nurture an abundance of self-confidence.

Chapter Twenty

Conscious and subconscious

'Of course it is happening inside your head, Harry, but why on earth should that mean that it is not real?'
— ***Harry Potter and the Deathly Hallows***
(J.K. Rowling)

Explaining something as complex as consciousness always has and probably always will have scientists, theologians and philosophers baffled. The human brain is a highly complex organ, with over 100 billion cells connected to 10,000 other cells, with over 10 trillion nerve connections. And although science has made huge leaps in understanding which part of the brain does what, so far, it has not been able to explain how we create and experience feelings, thoughts and emotions. It remains a mystery. All we can be certain of is that we are indeed conscious! Without consciousness, we have no way of proving we, or anything else for that matter, truly exist.

Consciousness is a group of different states. Minute to minute, hour to hour, day to day, your consciousness moves through different levels of wakefulness and productivity. When you are asleep, for example, you will be unaware of most things going on around you, but will wake easily if the stimulus is strong enough. Conversely, if you have fainted or fallen into a coma, you are less easily aroused. When you are fully conscious, you are aware of most everything that is going on around you and can respond and react accordingly.

Can consciousness exist outside of the brain?

Throughout history, scientists, theologians and philosophers have also been at odds over whether or not life after death exists. Do we have a spirit or a soul, and does it live on after death? Are we a spirit having a human experience, or a human having a spiritual experience?

The ancient Egyptians were never in any doubt about there being life after death. If you were poor, you were probably buried in the sand with whatever possessions you held dear, in order that you would be reunited with them in the afterlife. If you were wealthy, you would have been mummified, entombed with your valuables and, quite possibly, your entire household staff. Most Christians believe that after death, they will answer to God himself and be judged for the deeds they have done or failed to do during their lifetime. Buddhists believe that death is a natural part of the life cycle, and that it simply leads to rebirth.

I once read an interesting theory that if you think of your brain as a television, and consciousness as a satellite signal, when the TV breaks down (death occurs), surely the satellite signal is still emitting energy. If this is the case, perhaps we exist, at least in some form, after death. The debate will no doubt continue forever and a day, until the day that someone who has passed over comes back to enlighten the living.

Neuroscientists are of the opinion that because consciousness exists somewhere in the brain, without a brain there can be no consciousness. Ergo, if the brain dies, so does consciousness. Then, there is the theory of near-death experience (NDE). In a fascinating book, *Proof of Heaven*, a well-respected neurosurgeon named Eben Alexander writes of his own NDE. In it, he chronicles his journey into what he refers to as the *afterlife*, and by virtue of being someone who knows more than most about the human brain, his account, although a little 'out-there,' could perhaps be worth consideration.

I often wonder why we (myself included) need or like to have scientific proof before we can accept and really believe in something. When science tells us they have proven something, we are inclined to accept it as concrete. To have proof is to have finality. That is to say, *proof* is definitive, carved in stone, but as science has been proven wrong many times in the past, surely scientific *proof* is open to further conjecture.

Becoming more open-minded.

It is all very well to say you are open minded. I say this about myself, but just how open is your mind? Most of us have been brought up with belief systems based on other people's beliefs, such as our parents, caregivers, teachers, authority figures and so on. It is not until we get out into the big wide world that we begin to create our own set of beliefs, views and opinions based on our own life experiences. When we have a new experience, our world view can either change or remain unchanged. It is simply a matter of perception and flexibility. How flexible are you with your beliefs?

Not so long ago, my husband and I were enjoying dinner with some lovely friends when the light-hearted conversation turned to conspiracy theories, which in this instance, according to our friends, was less a theory and more a 'hard fact.' Now, I'll admit that I love a conspiracy theory; I'll even go as far as to confess that I've probably watched every episode of *Ancient Aliens*. However, as my children will testify, I am also a bit of a nerd, and so as much as you'll have my attention, my brain will also be scrambling around at 100 miles per hour, searching for logical explanations, preferably backed up by science. Although, science has been wrong about a lot of things, hasn't it?

Back to the conversation:

'Chem trails,' they said.

'Chem trails?' I repeated.

'You know, those plumes of smoke you see coming out the back of airplanes? They're toxic chemicals, or worse still, biological agents sprayed onto the earth's surface.'

'They're clouds of condensation, though.'

'No, they are toxic chemicals.'

'Who would spray these chemicals?'

'Oh, the government, the military, climate scientists, pharmaceutical companies, pilots...'

'Pilots?'

'Well, there's big money in it.'

'In what, exactly?'

'Weather control, keeping the population down, secret experiments – that sort of thing.'

'But the same people that spray these chemicals breathe the same air and are exposed to the same weather as the rest of us.'

'Yes, but they know how to stay safe.'

'Right, but you know this is really just water vapour turning to ice when it meets cold air?'

'Listen, when we're on the beach in the Caribbean, we don't see them at all, not one.'

'Case in point.'

'Trust me, it's a fact, and you'll notice them more now that you actually know the truth.'

'I don't think so.'

'Yes, you will.'

I have a tendency to get a bit prickly when anyone presents a firm and unwavering opinion that leaves no room for discussion.

'I definitely won't.'

'Oh yes, you will.'

'No, I won't."

Conversation moves awkwardly along.

Good food, plenty of wine and, of course, great friendships, and all is forgotten... or is it?

Fast forward to the following morning:

Me, Googling Chem Trails like there's no tomorrow, and reaching for the binoculars.

A superficial example of having (or pretending to have) an open mind perhaps, but being able to change our mind is what makes us humans so wonderfully unique. And for the record, no. Upon further research, I will not be joining the ranks of the Chem Trail conspiracy theorists any time soon.

There is a lot to be gained from opening your mind and letting in some fresh air: new ideas, new information and maybe even inspiration. I am not suggesting you start questioning everything you believe in, but perhaps consider being less rigid, as remaining open to ideas and new possibilities can be positively life-changing. Life is, after all, an incredible journey if you allow yourself to become a traveller rather than a bystander.

My little granddaughter said to me recently, 'Nana, do you know what's worse than being a bully?'

'No,' I said, 'tell me.'

'Being a bystander,' she replied.

Out of the mouths of babes.

Tips on keeping an open mind

1. Listen. Rather than listening, we are often preoccupied thinking about our reply.

2. Pause. Think about the possibilities rather than the likelihood.

3. Accept change. Like it or not, things change, we progress and we move forward. It's called evolution.

4. Stop controlling, or trying to control. Sometimes, just letting go and letting be can be a liberation in itself.

5. Allow yourself to make mistakes and accept that others make them, too. We are all, every one of us, perfectly imperfect.

6. Be present. Stop once in a while and just breathe. There really are enough hours in a day, and if you run out of hours in your day, go to sleep and begin again tomorrow.

7. Stop judging. Unless you are a judge or a barrister, reserve judgement of others.

8. Get curious. The world is full of wonders to behold, advancements to be had and obstacles to be overcome. Curiosity itself has never killed anyone, let alone a cat.

9. Stay calm. Not only does it feel good, but it conserves an abundance of energy which you can put to good use focussing on the things that make you feel good.

10. Read less... media. Experience life through your own eyes, not someone else's.

Chapter Twenty-One

What lies beneath?

'We all have two minds – conscious and subconscious. 95% of your life is controlled by your subconscious mind / your programming.'
– Dr Bruce Lipton, cell biologist

My husband and I travelled through Thailand recently, and stopped off to visit the Golden Buddha in Bangkok. The statue, known as *Phra Phuttha Maha Suwana Patimakon*, is a wonder to behold, and the story that goes with it is just as precious.

It is said that when the Burmese invaded the ancient city of Ayutthaya in the 1700s, the invaders looted and destroyed everything of value they could lay their hands on. The Buddhist monks, who wanted to keep their treasured effigies from being pilfered and defiled, covered the statue in clay, and so it remained untouched for hundreds of years, until one day in 1955, when it was moved to a new location. There are various accounts of exactly what happened next, but what is known for sure is that during the relocation, the statue accidently dropped to the ground and a large crack appeared. As repairs were about to start, one of the monks noticed a glint through the crack, and so they began to chip away carefully to see what lay beneath. The more they chiselled and chipped away, the more excited they became until finally a solid gold statue of Buddha was unveiled.

Freud's interpretation of the conscious and unconscious mind was depicted as an iceberg; the tip of the iceberg representing consciousness, and the huge berg beneath being the unconscious or subconscious.

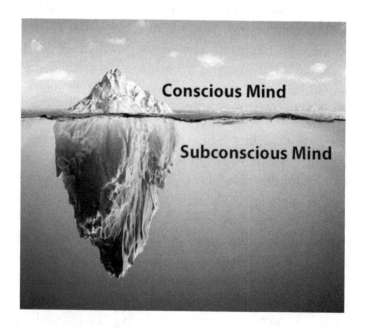

Brain activity is identified as conscious, meaning under intentional control, and everything else is referred to as unconscious or subconscious activity. It is easy to think that we live our lives consciously, even though most of the time we are moving through life with little conscious effort. We can think, walk, talk, move, see, hear, taste and smell all at the same time, and most of that is carried out unconsciously. In fact, the majority of the time, our life is being handled without our conscious intervention. The details of our lives are handled unconsciously, while we leisurely travel along.

Our subconscious mind takes care of us. It makes sure that we breathe, and that the air we inhale oxygenates the blood that surges through our brain and body. It keeps our heart beating, regulates our body temperature, makes our hair and our finger and toenails grow. It digests our food, delivers nutrients where they need to go and waste where it needs to go. It alerts our immune system to foreign invaders and creates new cells by the billions, 24 hours a day. Our subconscious mind stores memories, encodes and recalls them. This is all part of our autonomic nervous system.

So, if all of this, and more, is taken care of automatically, how is it possible to control it?

Take, for instance, your breath. Now, you do not have to remind yourself to breathe. It happens all by itself, and yet you can control it. You can breathe deeply, slowly, quickly, in or out, through your nose or mouth; you can hold your breath until you faint, if you like; you can use it to blow bubbles, whistle, sing, play an instrument, yawn, shout, whisper and probably much more, but now I am out of breath!

By breathing deeply and slowly into your diaphragm, you can lower your blood pressure (autonomic), slow your heart rate (autonomic), increase oxygenation (autonomic) and release endorphins, oxytocin, serotonin and dopamine (all autonomic). If this is not the epitome of mind over matter, I am not sure what is.

'Your mind is a garden, your thoughts are the seed, you can grow flowers or you can grow weeds.' – Anon

We know that the subconscious mind responds to repetition. Your conscious mind likes to learn new skills, and when those skills are repeated often enough, you create new neural pathways, i.e. new programming. If you heard a beautiful song, would you want to hear it again? Of course you would. You would want to hear it again and again because it made your heart sing. Listen to it often enough, and you will memorise the words without even realising it, and soon enough you know the song so well that you only need to hear the opening few bars before you recognise it. Your subconscious mind has recorded not only the words and music to the song, but the emotion you feel when you listen to it. No doubt, if you heard that song again 20 years from now, you would sing along word-perfect.

Let's assume you go to a bookstore, pick up an amazing self-help book and read it front to back. Your conscious mind enjoyed it – it likes new information – but what next? Your subconscious mind has not learned much, if anything, as no repetition has been involved. You would have to read the book, or at least the chapters of interest, and then put into practise what you have learned. This is how you reprogramme the subconscious mind.

I have heard so many people say things like:

'I read this great book once about how to lose weight.'

'Did it work?'

'Not really.'

'How many times did you read it?'

'Just the once. I don't think it was my kind of thing.'

Or:

'I went on this amazing course over the weekend and learned how to meditate.'

'How often do you meditate?'

'Oh, I can never find the time, but it was a great weekend.'

We live in the age of speed. Fast food, instant messaging, speed dating, swipe left, swipe right, quick fixes... We live our lives in such a hurry that we are in danger of missing much of it. The bottom line is that if you want change – *really* want change – you decide on it and you take action on it. You practise this new way of living your life until it becomes a habit, a pattern, and after a very short time, this is how and who you are. If there was a pot of gold at the end of a rainbow, and with a little patience and determination you could reach it in a matter of months, would you go after it or would you watch from the comfort of your armchair and wish for it?

Just imagine

'Imagination is more important than knowledge. Knowledge is limited. Imagination encircles the world.' – Albert Einstein

Whatever you want in your life, you must first imagine it. Everything begins here, in your imagination. Once you have a clear picture in your mind, you need to focus on it, often. The more attention you put on the things you want in your life, the more energy surrounds it, and so the more likely you are to attract it. Welcome back, Law of Attraction.

In a previous chapter we looked at visualisation and how everything that ever was and is began as a thought, idea or vision. You would be forgiven for thinking that visualising and imagining are one of the same, but there are subtle differences between the two.

In order to visualise something, you need to have a memory, experience or previous knowledge of that which you are visualising. So, if I were to suggest that you visualise hugging someone you love, or biting into a juicy red apple, your subconscious mind would quickly delve into your long-term memory and come up with a vivid picture of whatever that looks like (or has looked like) to you. On the other hand, if I were to suggest you *imagine* what it would feel like to ride on the shoulders of the abominable snowman, or ask how you would spend £100 million, unless you have experienced either of those things, you would have to use your imagination.

Let's take the Wright brothers. These two young bicycle mechanics from Dayton, Ohio, were born in the late 1800s, when the closest thing to man being able to fly involved strapping wings to your arms and take a leap of faith. We can go back even further, to the great Leonardo di Vinci, who designed a variety of flying machines as far back as 1488. Now, these men could not have just visualised a flying machine, because nothing of its kind had been created, so they would have used their imagination.

Tim Berners-Lee invented the World Wide Web, Bill Gates Microsoft and Steve Jobs the iPhone, all of which began in their imagination.

In hypnotherapy, we encourage the use of both visualisation and imagination. Imagining the desired feeling, event or circumstance as if it were already happening, and then visualising the steps you need to take in order to bring it into reality. Your reality.

Who do you think you are anyway?

Tongue in cheek, but a serious question nonetheless. There is a programme on television called *Who Do You Think You Are?* which delves into the ancestry of celebrities who want to know more about their family tree. I recall a delightful episode where the UK's own Danny Dyer discovered he was a direct descendant of William the Conqueror. More and more people are using ancestry websites to trace their lineage, and, more recently, sending off samples of DNA to analyse their entire genome. I have friends who have been thrilled to learn that they are 30% Native American or 25% Asian or 10% Icelandic, and I really do get it. It is fascinating stuff, and although I have no immediate plans to try it myself, I would not be at all surprised if one day I ended up sending my spittle off in a plastic test tube for a full analysis.

A few years ago, the BBC commissioned a programme called *The Incredible Human Journey*, based on the book of the same name by Dr Alice Roberts. The programme traced the history of human evolution, with Dr Roberts introducing the theory that modern humans all share a common ancestor. This ancestor lived around 195,000 years ago in Africa, most likely modern Ethiopia, and consequently we all share a fragment of the original DNA. There are, of course, other theorists out there that disagree with Dr Roberts's research, however, what is not argued is that humans are one species. This being the case, why are we all so different?

Self-awareness

'Nosce te Ipsum,' or 'Know thyself.' Wise words inscribed at the entrance of the Temple of Apollo at Delphi.

To be self-aware is to have knowledge of your character and feelings, and how they are perceived by others. This can be a good thing or something that can hold you back.

Let's assume you are at a party. You start telling a story, which at first has everyone's full attention. In your eyes, it is a riveting tale and one which you intend to milk for all it is worth. Halfway through the highly entertaining story, you realise you are labouring far too long and your audience are beginning to lose interest. Being self-aware, you may decide at this point to wrap it up and race ahead to the climax, saving face and crowd disbursement. If you are less self-aware, you may continue droning on until your audience have upped and left, leaving you feeling embarrassed, deflated and confused.

It's a balancing act

When you are self-aware, you are more confident and creative. You are more likely to feel empathy, be less judgemental and be more successful in your career and in your relationships. Someone who is less self-aware may doubt themselves, overthink things, over analyse their actions and be self-critical. These individuals may also find it difficult to accept criticism or blame.

My three top tips for becoming more self-aware:

1. Meditation

2. Hypnosis

3. Keeping a journal

The practise of meditation helps you to distance yourself from thoughts that persistently distract you.

Distraction is often a by-product of avoidance. For example, faced with uncomfortable thoughts or feelings, it is common to try to avoid thinking about them. By quietening the mind in meditation, you are more able to access those innermost thoughts safely, connect with the deeper feelings attached to those thoughts and face the things you need to do in order to move on or improve.

A more targeted approach would be to enlist the services of a professional clinical hypnotherapist. In hypnotherapy, we cut to the chase, using a variety of modalities, including EFT tapping and EMDR, to reprogramme unhelpful and outdated thinking patterns, and facilitate positive change.

Journaling is another option. I am a big fan of journaling. A journal can be used as a diary to write about your day, your mood and your deepest thoughts, as well as how you feel about yourself and others. It can be used as a goal-setting tool, and as a place to write and read positive affirmations. Studies have shown that putting feelings down on paper balances activity in the amygdala, the part of the brain responsible for controlling emotion.

Chapter Twenty-Two

Happiness

Happy, talky, talky, happy talk,
Talk about things you like to do,
You got to have a dream, if you don't have a dream,
How you gonna have a dream come true?
A song by Captain Sensible, 1982

Happiness is a feeling, a state of mind, and, this being the case, which it certainly is, it must be within our control to increase it.

Of course, happiness means different things to different people. I have seen programmes and news reports depicting people living in what we in the West would call third world or poverty-stricken conditions, yet, in front of the cameras at least, they laugh and smile and appear quite joyful. Many of these people have no money to buy goods and no access to clean water or education, so what is going on here? Could it be that their lives are somehow more meaningful? Perhaps it is because many people living in third world countries live more as a community, without personal agendas and overinflated egos. I am not talking here about countries with despot governments, who pillage and plunder their own people. I am simply taking a view on countries where people seem more satisfied with their lives.

I spent a lot of time immersed in local life on an island in the Eastern Caribbean. Life on the islands is generally relaxed and peaceful, and the people caring and friendly. With the exception of a few islands and islanders that have been infiltrated by drugs, gangs and crime, my personal experience has been that most people living on the islands are of a happy disposition. Many islanders still live in rickety chattel houses with outside toilets and wells for water, but the islands are lush with vegetation and fruit, and the oceans abundant with fish. It would be very difficult to live on an island like Grenada and go hungry; you would only have to venture down the road a little way before you came across a plant or a tree bearing ripe fruit. The pace of life is slow, no one is in a hurry, people stop to talk to one another and the markets are bustling with people dressed in vibrant colours selling and buying fresh produce, while men engage in lively games of dominos on the seafront and children run and play freely. That is not to say that all islanders are happy; there are those with problems certainly, and there are those that long for what they deem a better life, a richer life, in wealthier countries where the streets are apparently paved with gold. Those of us who live in these wealthy countries know full well that while there is indeed opportunity to become rich and successful, the streets are mostly dirty, and happiness is by no means guaranteed.

In wealthy countries, there is a huge divide between rich and poor, distinct social classes, a hierarchy and discrimination, all of which lead to fear, unrest, anger and depression. Although money is nice to have, it does not necessarily buy happiness. I can think of many high-profile celebrities who seem to have it all, and yet battle drug and alcohol addiction and suffer with low self-esteem, depression and anxiety. Sadly, many have gone on to take their own lives.

We hear stories of lottery winners who win millions vowing their lives will never change; some divorce or fall out with family members, get scammed, runout of funds and find themselves broke and alone. Reality stars, once desperate for money and fame, rue the day their dreams of fame became... *reality*!

No matter how you feel right now, there is probably a time or a moment where you felt really happy. Perhaps you bought a new car, got a promotion at work or found that £20 note you thought you had lost months ago tucked away in your jeans pocket. You dream of taking an exotic holiday, changing career, finding the love of your life, receiving a windfall or doing something that you're certain would make you happy, and then one day, one of these things actually happens. Does it feel as good as you had imagined? If so, how long did the good feeling last?

Most of us will have gone through this cycle at one time or another, wishing with all our heart for something to happen, and then one fine day that something happens, and with time, the happiness boost diminishes. This is known as the Hedonic Treadmill, which is the theory that everyone has a baseline level of happiness that we return to time and time again, regardless of what happens to us.

Can you keep the bliss alive and get off the treadmill?

Well, apparently there are good reasons for the existence of the treadmill. One reason is that when an achievement has been attained, our standards and expectations move up a notch, and so we have to keep going in order to feel a similar buzz again. Let's say you move into a new house. You explore the rooms, relish in the space, go out and buy bits and bobs to adorn your new abode, and then, over time, you just become used to it. So used to it, in fact, that you hardly notice the positives anymore, and you may even begin to find faults. With fewer positive things to focus on, and fewer positive feelings to accompany them, the happiness frequency cannot be sustained. When positive experience is repetitive, you know what to expect, and so do not get the same kick out of it. Perhaps you have lost weight, changed your eating habits, given up smoking or drinking, and the results have not only felt wonderful, but new opportunities have begun to show up. New romance, new job, more money in your pocket and now your aspirations have increased. You want to look better, feel better and be better. Time for a new challenge, a new dream and new goals.

Try 'mixing things up a bit.' By changing one or two things, you can breathe new life into the experiences you once felt great about. Consider ways in which you can do things differently, and then ask yourself if you would feel better by doing it.

Research suggests that happiness is a combination of how satisfied you are with your life overall and how good you feel on a day-to-day basis. Research also suggests that if you focus too much on *trying* to feel good all the time, you will undermine your ability to feel good at all. As we all have the ability to control how we feel, with practise we can develop new habits in order to achieve a more satisfying and fulfilling life.

My top tips:

Smile

You have heard me say this before, and I will say it again.

Whether your smile is real or fake, do it more often. The more you smile, the more you feel like smiling. When you smile, your facial muscles contract, firing a signal back to the brain that stimulates your reward system and increases levels of happy hormones. When your brain feels happy, you smile, and when you smile, your brain feels happy.

Exercise

Exercise increases endorphins and all our other feel good chemicals. It reduces the stress hormone cortisol and adrenaline, and has been shown to reduce depression and anxiety. Does it have to be about going to the gym, sweating buckets in a spin class of pumping iron? If that makes you feel good, then yes. If not, take a leaf out of the *Blue Zone* book I mentioned earlier or just get out there with nature.

The great outdoors

Nature makes us happy. Being outdoors and at one with nature has a tremendous therapeutic effect. Neuroscience has shown that our brains respond differently in different environments. Walking through a city, a built-up or noisy area versus a walk in the park stimulates different parts of your brain. Your frontal lobe, the part of the brain engaged in navigating your way through modern life, deactivates a little when we are outdoors, and alpha waves, your calm but alert state, grow stronger.

Spend more time with loved ones

Quality time with the people, pets and animals you love is fundamental to your levels of happiness. A recent study of couples pre- and post-parenthood found that most parents will choose to forego flashy cars, expensive jewellery and designer clothes in favour of spending time with their children. Research has shown that pet owners and those who spend time in the company of animals have better psychological and physical health than non-owners. If there is no one to love, then socialise more. Spending time socialising with friends or making new acquaintances can increase your sense of belonging, reduce stress by lifting your mood and help to overcome traumas and periods of sadness. And if you prefer your own company...

Read

The wisdom of the world is available to you. The French novelist, Marcel Proust, said reading is 'that fruitful miracle of a communication in the midst of solitude.' Reading (fiction in particular) increases empathy and social skills, and allows your mind to wander and expand. Reading improves brain circuitry and increases memory. You are in a Theta brain state while absorbed in a good book, which of course is a hypnotic state and your gateway to learning, memory and intuition.

Step away from your phone

Time is precious, so waste it wisely. Unless you are making calls to people who uplift you, start to become more aware of how much time you spend on or checking your phone. How many out-of-office calls do you make that you could make the following day during office hours? Put down the tech once in a while, and do more of the things that hold your interest and make you forget to keep checking your phone.

Embrace your age

Our younger years are said to be the best years of our lives, but there are plenty of reasons to look forward to maturity. More life experience means more wisdom, more skills and perhaps even more happiness. A study from the London School of Economics concluded that people are the happiest between the ages of 20 to 70, with our joy peaking at the ages of 23 and 69. That's a wide window for happiness!

Sleep more

A well-rested brain is a happy brain. A good night's sleep is fundamental to your sense of happiness and wellbeing. Anyone who has ever experienced a bad night's sleep will know that an exhausted person is not a happy one. People who get insufficient sleep are more likely to experience negative thoughts and suffer from depression. Now, there will be some of you reading this right now saying, 'Oh, I get by on a couple of hours a night and I'm doing fine.' If this is you, you may be one of life's 'short sleepers,' and although there are studies that show a small proportion of short sleepers are *true* short sleepers, the majority of people who have insufficient sleep will be chronically sleep-deprived without realising it.

Altruism

An old Chinese saying goes: 'If you want happiness for an hour, take a nap. If you want happiness for a day, go fishing. If you want happiness for a year, inherit a fortune. If you want happiness for a lifetime, help somebody.'

MRI scans on the brain have shown that the act of giving activates the same parts of the brain that are stimulated by food and sex. Woo hoo! Evidence shows that altruism is hardwired in the brain, and it produces that lovely feel-good chemical dopamine. Helping others may just be the secret to living a life that is not only happier, but also healthier, wealthier, more productive and more meaningful.

Gratitude

I know, I know, I'm repeating myself, but gratitude is a big deal these days and rightly so, as it has been shown that it can improve both physical and psychological health. People who show gratitude report fewer aches and pains, a general feeling of overall good health and take more regular exercise than those who do not. Grateful people enjoy a greater sense of wellbeing and happiness, and suffer less from anxiety and depression. When you are feeling grateful, you are less likely to feel vengeful or bitter, and are more likely to behave in a pro-social manner with sensitivity and empathy.

The way to a beautiful life

What is your idea of a beautiful life?

In this, I urge you to be specific. Simply stating 'health, wealth and happiness' is not sufficient, because these are just words with broad meanings. I pose this burning question along the same lines as the 'why are we here?' or 'where did we come from?' kind of question.

And then, ask yourself:

- 'What can I do to achieve the things that would make my life beautiful?'

- 'What needs to change?'

- 'What can I do today that would be easy for me to change?'

If you pay close attention, you will notice plenty of people who play the blame game. 'It's not my fault that my life is like it is. It's the government's fault, it's my upbringing, my family – it's the fault of my colleagues, my boss, the weather, the economy, lack of education, lack of opportunity... life is not fair, life is hard.'

And then we have the *if-only* types. 'If only I had more money, more opportunity, more knowledge, more friends in high places, a kick-start, a leg-up, a hand-out, a loving partner, a home of my own, a good job, better looks,' and so on. The list is endless.

What if we were to spend our lives waiting for the things around us to change? What then?

Climate change. We can sit around in the hope the climate eventually accepts the way we humans do things, or we change the way we do things! When democratically-elected governments fail to deliver on their promises, we do not leave them in office forevermore, we move to change. If there had been no civil rights movement, no votes for women and no fight against Hitler; if we sat back and accepted terrorism or communism, where would we all be? We make changes, it is what we do.

What this boils down to is that the only thing you can *control* is YOU. How you think, how you respond, how you react, how you feel and how you interpret the world you live in; what you believe, what you value, your choices and decisions; whether you go left or right, forward or backwards; stay stuck in the past or embrace the future. All you have is YOU. If you are happy and content, then there is nothing more you need to do. If, however, you want something else, something more, make some changes!

Is change really that simple?

Let's get back onto the subject of personal change, not global change. I was merely making (some may argue labouring) a point.

Netflix aired a series in 2019, *Living with Yourself*. This was a light-hearted show exploring the idea of human perfection and what might happen if it we could edit out our flaws. The programme chronicled the life of a middle-aged man in the depths of a midlife crisis. Upon the recommendation of a friend and colleague, who is going from strength to strength, he visits a spa on an abandoned strip mall, where two mysterious men assure him of his pending perfection. As it turns out, the perfect version of a human is a perfectly edited clone. The original version is unceremoniously disposed of, and the new improved version picks up the proverbial baton. In the character's case, the cloning is a success aside from one major flaw, as a glitch in the procedure results in both the old and new versions being alive and well, living with themselves.

The concept of cloning is nothing new. Dolly the Sheep was the first mammal to be cloned back in 1996, and more recently, researchers have successfully cloned the human embryo, as unsettling as that may be. Clones also occur naturally, as in the case of identical twins, who are genetic copies with identical DNA. If you had the opportunity to become a perfect version of yourself, how far would you be willing to go? Interesting dinner party conversation perhaps?

As far as I am aware, no one has been so bold as to state and then go on to prove that life is easy. You will always have ups and downs, yins and yangs, and bumps in the road. Life is full of surprises, and you can never know with certainty what lies around the corner. These are the facts. Benjamin Franklin once said there were only two things certain in life: death and taxes. Correct me if I am wrong, but not everyone pays tax. So, I would say there are two things certain in life: living a full life or living a half-life.

I am reminded of a short story by Leo Tolstoy, *The Death of Ivan Ilyich.* Ivan was a self-absorbed man who spent his life climbing the social ladder. Trapped in an unhappy marriage, he hated his wife and daughter, and so focussed on work rather than family. Ivan himself said that his life was, 'most simple and most ordinary and therefore most terrible.' On his deathbed, he asked his wife this question, 'What if my whole life has been wrong?' A sad tale with an even more miserable ending.

Years ago, as an investment broker in London, I attended dozens of lectures, conferences, talks and seminars on the subject of change. Most were based on the *Kübler Ross Change Curve*, which consists of five stages, often referred to as the five stages of grief:

1. Denial

2. Anger

3. Bargaining

4. Depression

5. Acceptance

As a change management process, these five steps are whittled down to four phases:

1. Denial

2. Anger

3. Exploration

4. Acceptance

Change can be an unsettling time; it can introduce uncertainty and fear. You may not want change, or you may not feel comfortable with it. Change puts you outside of your comfort zone, and as the creatures of habit that we are, we become fond of our comfort zones, like a comfy old pair of slippers.

Imagine that you have been wearing the same pair of slippers for a while; they are worn in and fit your feet like a pair of cosy mittens. They look familiar and they feel familiar. They have become a bit baggy and loose over time, a few bald patches have appeared, the dog might have had a chew, and you might have taken the rubbish out while wearing them or even popped to the corner shop. They have probably been in the washing machine a few times and the colour has faded, but they are your comfy old slippers. One day, you slip them on, and your big toe goes straight through. A new pair of slippers are now in the offing. You try to sew them up, patch them and tape them, but nothing works. You try walking barefoot around the house for a few days, skid about in socks and try to convince yourself that you can go without slippers altogether. You finally give in, admit to yourself that you need new slippers and you set off for the shop. You gasp in disbelief at the price and refuse to invest at first. With a sullen face, you find a suitable pair, try them on for size and begrudgingly take them over to the till. You walk away with an unfamiliar pair of slippers, which you are sure will never match up to the old ones. When you get home, you put them on, and while they are not quite as comfy, they are nonetheless pleasantly comfy. Instead of flopping about like mittens, they fit like gloves. You may even answer the door to the postman in complete confidence now that you have footwear to be proud of. The old slippers are no more. Change has occurred and it was not so bad after all. You just needed time to adjust.

Now, this may appear a flippant example of change, but the use of metaphor plays a vital role in hypnotherapy and other therapeutic modalities for change. Metaphor is an integral part of language and cognition; it is a central way in which we understand our world, and more importantly, our own inner experiences. Before humans devised the art of writing, we told stories. Wonderfully vivacious tales containing wisdom, lessons, meaning and morals. This is the language of the subconscious mind. Your subconscious mind is not logical or analytical; it uses the language of symbols, pictures and metaphors to communicate new ideas to your conscious mind. New ideas! Inspiration!

What can you do today that would be easy for you to change?

You can make a small change right now, or a big change starting today by taking small steps. There is no need (unless you are of the mind) to go headfirst into a monumental shift. You could end up shocking yourself and those around you. Bear in mind, it may not be just you that goes through the stages of change, it could be your family, friends or your work colleagues who put up the resistance.

Always remember, it is not possible to control the thoughts and actions of others, so if you come across resistance from others, perhaps by putting doubt in your mind with their own negative comments or opinions, you can either choose to let their beliefs control you, or you can move on past and continue along your own personal journey of self-improvement. You are the only one living your life, and despite other people's often well-meaning interference, only you know what your heart truly desires. Some ideas and, hopefully, inspiration as to how you can discover your heart's desire are laid out in this book. You can be the traveller, the explorer and the adventurer on your journey through life, or you can be a passenger hitching a ride in someone else's car.

There is a way to a beautiful life, and finding it may not be as difficult as you think.

CPSIA information can be obtained
at www.ICGtesting.com
Printed in the USA
BVHW041507240720
584626BV00002B/5

9 781913 479343